CAN I SEE YOUR I.D.?

TRUE STORIES OF FALSE IDENTITIES

BY **CHRIS BARTON**
ILLUSTRATIONS BY **PAUL HOPPE**

DIAL BOOKS
an imprint of Penguin Group (USA) Inc.

DIAL BOOKS
An imprint of Penguin Group (USA) Inc.
Published by The Penguin Group
Penguin Group (USA) Inc., 375 Hudson Street,
New York, NY 10014, U.S.A.
Penguin Group (Canada), 90 Eglinton Avenue East, Suite 700,
Toronto, Ontario, Canada M4P 2Y3
(a division of Pearson Penguin Canada Inc.)
Penguin Books Ltd, 80 Strand, London WC2R 0RL, England
Penguin Ireland, 25 St. Stephen's Green, Dublin 2, Ireland
(a division of Penguin Books Ltd)
Penguin Group (Australia), 250 Camberwell Road,
Camberwell, Victoria 3124, Australia
(a division of Pearson Australia Group Pty Ltd)
Penguin Books India Pvt Ltd, 11 Community Centre,
Panchsheel Park, New Delhi - 110 017, India
Penguin Group (NZ), 67 Apollo Drive, Rosedale, North Shore 0632,
New Zealand (a division of Pearson New Zealand Ltd)
Penguin Books (South Africa) (Pty) Ltd, 24 Sturdee Avenue,
Rosebank, Johannesburg 2196, South Africa
Penguin Books Ltd, Registered Offices: 80 Strand,
London WC2R 0RL, England

Designed by Jasmin Rubero
Text set in Apollo MT
Printed in the U.S.A.

1 3 5 7 9 10 8 6 4 2

Library of Congress Cataloging-in-Publication Data
Barton, Chris.
Can I see your I.D.? : true stories of false identities /
by Chris Barton ; illustrations by Paul Hoppe.
p. cm.
Includes bibliographical references.
ISBN 978-0-8037-3310-7 (hardcover)
1. Impostors and imposture—Biography—Juvenile literature.
2. False personation—Case studies—Juvenile literature. 3. Identity (Psychology)—
Case studies—Juvenile literature. I. Hoppe, Paul, ill. II. Title.
CT9980.B34 2011
001.9'5—dc22
2010011878

For Mom, Dad,
and Joe T. Moore
—C.B.

TABLE OF CONTENTS

KERON THOMAS 1

FERDINAND WALDO DEMARA JR. 13

PRIVATE WAKEMAN................................25

SOLOMON PEREL.................................35

FORREST CARTER 49

PRINCESS CARABOO..........................57

ELLEN CRAFT 71

JOHN HOWARD GRIFFIN 87

RILEY WESTON.............................95

FRANK W. ABAGNALE JR......................105

AFTERWORD................................113

ACKNOWLEDGMENTS 119

BIBLIOGRAPHY 123

SUBWAY MOTORMAN?
KERON THOMAS

SATURDAY, MAY 8, 1993
NEW YORK CITY

If there had been trains on the island of Trinidad, where you lived until you were twelve, you might have gotten your thing for them out of your system by now. But there weren't, and you didn't, and that's why you're here at the 207th Street subway station carrying a bag of motorman's tools and signing someone else's name.

If all goes well, they'll never know that your name is Keron Thomas and that you're sixteen. If all goes well, they'll believe you when you tell them that you're Regoberto Sabio, and they'll have no idea that he's supposed to be forty-four years old. You're a six-footer, but you can't pass for forty-four. Twenty-four, maybe. But not forty-four.

1

You met Sabio while you were hanging out on the Franklin Avenue Shuttle he operates weekday afternoons and evenings back in Brooklyn. You knew so much about the subway already that you didn't come off as suspiciously eager to learn more. In fact, you told Sabio you were a motorman too, on another line. Obviously, you were a young, single motorman with time on his hands and a need for a mentor. Why else would you have ridden his four-stop route back and forth in the cab with him for several hours each week since last winter?

In addition to the tools, you'd gotten your hands on this Transit Authority uniform shirt. You kept it in your bag at school, and you'd throw it on before you got to the Franklin Avenue station. Between that T.A. shirt and your calm, mature demeanor, nobody would look at you and see a teenage train fanatic. That allowed you to observe Sabio up close and learn a lot more than you could have while watching a motorman through a closed cab door.

You paid close attention to everything Sabio did. As he ran his train down the line and back, you picked up on the lingo from his radio chats with the tower. You watched him brake when he came into a station, saw how he eased the train back out again. He's a talkative guy, so there was a lot of conversation in there, a lot of advice. "Don't stay out drinking the night before you've got a shift," he'd tell you. "Don't let management tell you how to wear your hair," "Take notes on everything you do," and so forth. It was all professional advice, not technical, because he thought you already knew the mechanics of operating a train, right?

Somewhere along the way, you got the idea that you probably *did* know enough to drive the train. But you didn't want to just *know*—you wanted to *do*. And this week when Sabio mentioned that vacation he had coming up, you saw your chance.

You asked some questions not too surprising coming from a rookie motorman: Who's going to take your shift while you're out? Can I do it? How do I go about getting some overtime, anyway?

He said, "Call the crew office and see what they say."

Which you did.

Late last night.

In Sabio's name.

But you didn't ask for his Franklin Shuttle route. You told them what train you really wanted. Come on in, they told you. 207th Street station, they said. And here you are—where, most likely, nobody knows that the real Regoberto Sabio is not only much older than you but four inches shorter and forty pounds lighter. They probably don't know that he wears a beard or sports dreadlocks down past his waist.

"I'm the extra man," you tell the dispatcher. "You have a train for me?"

You sign in with Sabio's name—no pass code needed,

no Transit Authority I.D. required. You catch a little grief about the way you're dressed—you've got on your uniform shirt, but you're wearing jeans instead of the regulation blue trousers.

"Hey, you're not in your uniform pants," he says.

"They're at the cleaners," you say.

"I'll let you go today—it's the weekend."

He buys it. He believes you. You're in.

He issues you a big, bulky radio, and now you've got a train to drive.

You've studied hard for this day. Not in any classroom—Automotive High never has taught you what you most wanted to know—but in the stations scattered beneath the streets of the city, and on the trains thundering through them.

All your life, you've wanted to know how things work—the mechanics of them. What's inside a remote control that lets it run a toy car? The only way to find out is to open it up and see for yourself. And that's pretty much what you've done with the subway.

Long before you began hanging out with Sabio, you were riding the subway for fun on weekends, situated at the front of the train so you could get a peek at the tracks, see how the signals are working. Lots of kids do that, of course. But how many teenagers have train posters in their bedrooms? How many sing out "Next stop, Franklin" while pretending a piece of wood and a stapler are the controls? Or count *Rules and Regula-*

tions Governing Employees Engaged in the Operation of the New York City Transit System among their favorite books?

Becoming one of those employees after you graduate would be great—but you're impatient. Why wait until then to drive a train when you see a way you can do it *now*?

When the dispatcher told you to report way up at 207th, it could mean only one thing: You got the train you asked for. *The A.* You've hit the jackpot. The A train is the longest line in the system. You've heard it's also one of the hardest lines for a beginning operator to learn on, because it involves lots of switching on and off different tracks. That's good. You want a little challenge.

You're not stealing the train, any more than someone can steal an escalator—it's going to come right back to where you got it, isn't it? At least, that's how you see it as you walk out onto the platform with your bag containing a motorman's two main tools—a brake handle and a reverser key—along with a Day-Glo orange safety vest.

You do like you've seen Sabio do—charge up the air compressors that power the brakes, walk through the train, make sure everything's in order. Then you step into the cab and wait for the conductor to give you two long buzzes. You give him two short ones in reply. It's 3:58 p.m.—time to go.

Sabio's shuttle is just two cars long, but the A has

eight—that's six hundred feet of train. The controls are also different from the ones you've watched Sabio operate, but that's all right. You'll figure them out. All you need to do is just—

Uh-oh.

The train starts to move backward. That's *never* supposed to happen. You put on the brake, but not before you feel the train nudge the bumping block behind it. Hoping nobody noticed, you reverse direction and pull out of the station.

You accelerate.

You're in control. You're used to the rattle and the clatter and the whine of the trains, but this power, this exhilaration—this feeling is new, and you've never known anything better. You *knew* you could do it. You feel like a pro.

This train is taking you—no, *you're* taking *it*—the entire length of Manhattan, clear across Brooklyn, and all the way out to Lefferts Boulevard on the edge of Queens. Running time: about an hour fifteen. You'll haul hundreds of passengers, maybe thousands—none of them with any idea who's behind this cab door. They're a trusting bunch—not trusting in *you*, exactly, but in the T.A. You know what you're doing, though, so they're in good hands all the same.

When you get to Lefferts, you need to change onto a Brooklyn-bound train. But you can't get your radio out of the cab—that requires a key that you don't have. On the platform, you spot another motorman.

"Hey, can I borrow your radio key?" you ask. "I lost mine."

"Yeah, no problem!" he says.

Radio removed and complication resolved, you slide into the cab of your next train for your return to 207th Street. Back you go, easing into and out of the stations at Euclid Avenue, Jay Street, Fulton, World Trade Center, Washington Square, Penn Station, Forty-second Street, and on up Eighth Avenue.

The switches aren't a problem—no problem at all. You've got them down. In the past two and a half hours, you've made all eighty stops on time, with only five more to go on this round trip. Then you get to do it again.

North of the 168th Street station, there's a downgrade and a speed limit of twenty mph. You've got your train under that, but you pick up speed on the decline, and by the time you see the red signal warning that you're going too fast, it's too late. The emergency brake system kicks in, and the train—*your* train, all 360 tons of it—groans to a halt.

Now what? Ordinarily, a motorman would get out of the cab, go down onto the tracks, reach under the train to manually reset the brake, and be on his way.

The problem is, you're missing a key piece of equipment: a flashlight. And while there's some light down in the tunnel, it's not enough to suit you. Without some serious illumination, there's just no way you're going to get down there and feel around and risk getting yourself fried by those 625 volts coursing through the third rail. No. Way.

Instead, you radio in to the tower and tell them you can't get the brake to reset. "I'm in BIE," you say. "Send me out an RCI." Brakes in emergency. Road car inspector. You read about them in a book.

After what seems like forever stuck there just south of 175th Street, an inspector comes through the tunnel, resets the brake, and you're off again. Soon, you limp back into the 207th Street station, where a dispatcher and supervisor are waiting for you.

Standard procedure says that when a motorman breaks the speed limit, he gets taken downtown to get tested for drugs and booze. Gotta keep the subway safe, you know.

The T.A. supervisor gets back on the A with you for the forty-five-minute ride back to headquarters on Jay Street in Brooklyn. Along the way, you've got a lot to think about. The thing you think about the most is this: You really, really don't want to go in there.

So you don't. You emerge from the Jay Street station, up the stairs and onto the street. But instead of making the short walk to T.A. headquarters, you tell the supervisor, "You know what? I don't think I want to take this test."

"You could lose your job," he says. "Just take the test. If you weren't drinking, then it's nothing to worry about."

"It's a little more than that," you reply. And then you're gone.

Not on foot. Not on a bus. Not in a taxi.

You go right back down into the Jay Street station, and you're on a train in nothing flat. How else are you gonna get home?

WHAT HAPPENED NEXT?

KERON THOMAS was tracked down and arrested two days after his escapade on the A train, which made national headlines. "[W]hat Mr. Thomas did is monumental," wrote one newspaper columnist. "Reprehensible, to be sure, but decidedly awesome, bodacious." He was sentenced to three years' probation and for a while continued hoping to become a (legitimate) train operator. But, he says, those hours at the helm of the A train got the subway bug out of his system. Today, he does make his living in the transportation business—but by driving a truck, not a train.

NAVY SURGEON?
FERDINAND WALDO DEMARA JR.

TUESDAY, MARCH 13, 1951
SAINT JOHN, NEW BRUNSWICK, CANADA

Less than a week ago, you were known by the Brothers of Christian Instruction as Brother John Payne, and they knew you to have been Cecil Boyce Hamann before you entered their order.

But that was before those ungrateful so-and-sos passed you over for a plum role at the new Catholic college that you practically founded for them. So on March 10 you left them and Alfred, Maine, behind. For that matter, so did their car, which you took for your trip down to Boston.

In those 100 miles, you became Dr. Joseph Cyr— that's the name you checked in under at your hotel.

And after turning right back around, driving past Alfred and the rest of Maine up north to Saint John, that's also the name that you've just used to score a commission into the Royal Canadian Navy.

You're now a surgeon lieutenant in the second year of the Korean War. You're also Ferdinand Waldo Demara Jr., high school dropout from Lawrence, Massachusetts.

SPRING 1951
HALIFAX, NOVA SCOTIA, CANADA

Even traveled directly, it's quite a ways from Lawrence to the Stadacona naval base in Halifax. But you, Demara— ever since you left home after your junior year at Central Catholic High School to try your hand at a monk's life, you've never traveled directly. In the thirteen years since, you've never stuck to the accepted path or the proper channels.

And why would you? Your father did things the "right" way—he worked hard, built a buisness, got a nice house. And look what it got him: He lost the business during the Depression, moved your family from Prospect Hill to South Lawrence, and took a job as a movie theater projectionist.

Your big sister did things the right way too. Got married at St. Patrick's Cathedral to an Ivy Leaguer, a

Brown University man. Became a nurse. She died of a head injury three years ago, when she was just twenty-nine. So much for the rewards of the right way.

So the road that has led you to Stadacona has been one of your own design and choosing, a road paved by an impatient desire to have others recognize the greatness you've seen in yourself all the while. Along the way, your vehicles of choice have been new names and identities. At first, the church created them for you—here, you were Frater Mary Jerome; there, Brother John Berchmans—but eventually you began to borrow others'. Most recently, of course, it was the identity of your good friend, young Dr. Cyr.

You weren't hurting anybody. In fact, really, you've always been out to help, to share your impressive talents and energy and intellect with the world. But clashing with abbots, downing barrels of beer, going AWOL from the U.S. Army, and faking suicide to get out of the U.S. Navy made it a bit difficult to bestow those gifts as Fred Demara. So you took to borrowing birth certificates and academic credentials and writing letters of recommendation for yourself on official stationery you'd swiped.

Each new guise gave you a new opportunity to help people. They also allowed you to learn a lot about how big institutions work. You've seen the church, the military, hospitals, and universities from the inside. You've seen their big shots up close, and frankly, you're not impressed. You've sat through their unpronounceable theology courses and read through their boring law textbooks, and one thing's for sure: They're no better than a C student from Central Catholic.

You know just how to play them:

1. There's always plenty of power to be grabbed in one of those institutions, so long as you don't step on the toes of someone who's already got a little power of his own.

2. If anyone questions you, don't defend—attack; put the burden of proof on him.

3. Flattery and deference will get you everywhere.

This particular moment offers a pristine example of that last point. See, before volunteering for duty, you had no time to cram for your new role as Navy doctor, no opportunity to stuff your head with information gleaned from medical textbooks. You're equipped only with the details dropped last winter by the real—and completely unsuspecting—Dr. Cyr in his casual conversations with you. That, and your own good sense.

Here at the base, your duties include handling sick call each morning. Several thousand miles from the front, you expect the action to be relatively light, but you could still use a little help. So you mentioned to your superior officer that you've been asked to take on a side project—putting together a do-it-yourself medical guide for the doctorless fellows at an isolated lumber camp out in British Columbia. Would he like to help?

Would he? And how. Like it does every time, buttering up an expert by asking for his opinion worked like a charm. Your superior ran with the project, practically took the whole thing out of your hands, and did it himself.

And now he presents you with a booklet guaranteed to get someone with zero medical training up to speed on treating the everyday injuries and ailments they might encounter around a bunch of loggers—or sailors.

Between that booklet and your access to an ample supply of antibiotics, you're all set.

JULY 1951
PACIFIC OCEAN

Well, here's a situation that the lumber camp guide doesn't cover, and for which penicillin is no help at all.

You're the medical officer on the HMCS *Cayuga*, a destroyer making her way from Hawaii to Guam en route to her second tour of duty in Korea. You're days away from your destination, and someone needs a rotten tooth pulled.

And it's not just anyone. It's the captain himself.

You arrive at his cabin late in this summer day to have a look, and it's obvious that the old man is suffering. It's also obvious that he expects Doc Cyr to be able to do something about it.

While you get your bearings, you ask him a few questions. Turns out, Captain Plomer was scheduled to get the tooth yanked before the *Cayuga* went to sea, but he was too busy, it wasn't bothering him much, etc., etc. That's good to know—it means he bears responsibility for the situation, which means he should be willing to cut you some slack as you figure out how best to handle it.

You have him open his mouth, and you peer inside. Teeth look a lot alike, and they sure are close together, but this one back here seems to be the one that's troubling the old man—you think.

You tell Captain Plomer, quite correctly, that you did not learn a thing about dentistry in medical school. You can pull the bad tooth, but not until morning. At the moment, you can give him some pills for the pain, but you need some time to prepare if you're going to do this right.

It's a long night back in your cabin. In all the medical books on board—and you've looked, and looked, and looked—there's next to nothing about pulling teeth. What little you find, you read over and over. And you wonder what will happen to you if, out here in the middle of the Pacific, you botch this procedure on the man who runs the *Cayuga*. If ever there was a time when you needed a drink . . .

Morning comes, ready or not, and the captain wants you down in his day cabin now. He wants to get this over with, and as much as you do too, you haven't managed to work up much enthusiasm for it. Still, you grab your bag, go over in your head what needs to happen, and head down to your makeshift dentist's office.

And when you get there . . . everything goes like a dream. With an audience watching through the ammunition chute overhead, you stick a needle full of Novocain into the old man's gums. What's the right amount? You don't know, but you're inclined to err on the side of freezing half his face. Once he's good and numb, you take what appears to be the right tool, grab hold of what appears to be the right tooth, give it a pull, and become a hero.

The tooth is out, the captain is happy, and you feel like there's nothing Doc Cyr can't handle.

MONDAY, SEPTEMBER 10, 1951
KOREA BAY

And as it turns out, the *Cayuga*'s medical officer doesn't see a whole lot more action than a doctor back at Stadacona does. There are bruises, cuts, and steam burns, but those can be handled just as easily by your assistant, Petty Officer Hotchin.

Your main jobs on the ship are keeping an eye out for morale problems and, not entirely unrelated, dispensing the rum rations. As the so-called "morale officer," you make the rounds in your dress whites, .45 automatic pistol (an unusual piece of equipment for a surgeon) strapped to your side, chatting up seamen on the lower decks and fellow officers up above.

Between your smiles and jokes, you don't mind talking about yourself one bit, and you easily deal with potentially dicey questions about your background. Such as: How is it that a fellow with the French Canadian name of Cyr, who originally hails from the French Canadian province of Quebec, has such a thick Massachusetts accent?

Why, that's simple, you tell them: You were educated in Boston. Lucky for you, nobody expects Doc Cyr to speak French, other than a couple of Quebecois boys in the kitchen, and who'll pay them any mind? You're both an officer and a doctor, and while you yourself aren't impressed by men's titles and degrees, you know that others are easily awed by those things.

As for the *Cayuga*'s role during these September days, the ship is supporting South Korean guerrillas during their raids on the western coast. The *Cayuga* rides the waves at a safe distance while shelling targets on the mainland. When you do see the sorts of injuries a lumber-camp manual might not cover, they're typically among the Koreans after one of their raids.

Today, the *Cayuga* is returning to the area where the most recent raids were staged a few days ago. When you get there, the Koreans waste no time sending a junk over to greet you—and with good reason.

There are six or seven wounded men on board, three of them in bad, bad shape. There's a chest wound, another shot in the groin, and a third just as bad off—and God knows how many hours or days they've been in this condition. You're called down to have a look and determine how best to handle them.

You don't need to be an expert to know that these men are going to die if they don't get operated on soon.

Whatever you had in mind that day you showed up with Joseph Cyr's credentials at the recruiting office in Saint John, it wasn't this. No matter. You've got a job to do.

And there's not room to do it in the sick bay. Even if there were, wielding a scalpel amid these waves, with those frail bodies lying on those narrow tables . . . ? Not a chance. You're going to do it right here on this steel deck, on blankets in the shade of the torpedo tubes.

Everyone scrambles to get you what you need. Your gear is here. Hotchin is here. There's no time to delay. First up is the chest wound. The only way to know exactly what damage the guy suffered is to open him up. There's no time to consult the literature back in your cabin. You just have to do it.

And so you scalpel your way down to the ribs, then cut through one of those. The next incision will collapse the lung, allowing a better look at the wound. Could Hotchin handle the collapse? Sure. But this one is yours.

While Hotchin attends to the others, you carry on. By the time he comes back, you've covered the wound with Gelfoam to stop the bleeding. You tell Hotchin, "I removed the bullet."

Anyone who knows you knows you'd be only too happy to show off that bullet. But you don't. You've got two other patients to tend to, Dr. Cyr.

WHAT HAPPENED NEXT?

FERDINAND WALDO DEMARA JR. agreed to let the Royal Canadian Navy distribute the story of Dr. Cyr's surgical heroics to the newspapers back in Canada. The real Dr. Joseph Cyr saw the coverage, and the Navy quickly discharged Demara, who went on to pose as a psychology teacher at a college in Washington State and a Texas prison warden, among other roles. As a California minister under his real name, he was welcomed at a *Cayuga* reunion in 1979. Demara died in 1982.

MAN IN UNIFORM?
PRIVATE WAKEMAN

THURSDAY, FEBRUARY 18, 1864
WASHINGTON, D.C.

Your marching orders finally came through, Private—right along with this cold snap. After sixteen months of watching this war against the Confederates from the safety of Washington and Northern Virginia, you're at last heading south to see the elephant, as they say.

Your commanders ordered you to be ready to move at a moment's notice, and for the soldiers of the 153rd New York Infantry, that moment is now. Out here in this freezing weather, you're lined up four abreast, a regiment full of volunteers. Each of you *chose* to enlist. None of you *had* to sign up for whatever now awaits you.

Especially not you, Rosetta.

You're a volunteer among volunteers. You, who could get out of this march, out of this Army, and out of this war at just half a moment's notice, simply by confessing that you're not really a man. You could be sure to miss the next Gettysburg, the next Chickamauga. But you like this life first-rate. It suits your independent nature.

The money's good too. When you left the family farm in Chenango County a year and a half ago, you also left behind all feminine limitation on how much you could earn. As a man, you snagged yourself a wage of five dollars for just a few days' work—hauling a barge of Pennsylvania coal up the Chenango Canal and then east on the Erie, clear over to Montgomery County. That's where you ran into the Union Army recruiters.

Five foot tall and nary a whisker? No matter. They offered you $152—nearly a whole year's pay—right up front for joining for three years, and thirteen dollars more every month after that. Well, that was a fine test of what kind of man you were. For what kind of man would pass up the opportunity to finish off this war and keep the Union together? Besides, what kind of living could you have earned once you got known as a man willing to shirk his honor and duty?

So you added two years to your actual age of nine-teen, and that was that—you were signed up. You stuck around Montgomery County for a couple of months until they'd filled in the ranks of the 153rd. And in October of 1862, you all mustered in and moved out, down to the captured rebel town of Alexandria, Virginia.

Some Union Army recruits have seen battle—and met their maker—less than two weeks after kissing their mothers good-bye. All these months of guarding and drilling in Alexandria and Washington have given you a chance to send many a letter home to your parents and eight younger sisters and brothers. Your family knows where you are, and what you've been doing. They've written faithfully in reply, addressing their letters to "R. L. Wakeman."

But no one in the Army is reading your mail, telling you what you can say or can't say about the 153rd or anything else. So while nobody in the barracks has known you as anything other than Private Lyons Wakeman, you've signed your letters home with "Rosetta Wakeman," "Sarah Rosetta," "Miss Rosetta," "Affectionate Sister," "Affectionate Daughter" . . .

In those letters, you haven't pretended to be anything you're not. You haven't pretended to be a man. You haven't *pretended* to be a soldier—you *are* a soldier. And you haven't pretended to be someone who can live at home with them again after the war ends, if you live to see it.

There's been no need for your letters home to rehash all those old tensions. *You* know what they were about, and *they* know it too. All that matters is that you know you had to leave. You don't ever intend to go back to stay, no more than you could have stuck around in the first place. A farm of your own on the Wisconsin prairie sounds good. That can be your prize for getting neither found out nor killed.

You might just get there with the help of these Army wages—they're yours, and you get to decide what to do with them. You've sent some home and told your folks how to divvy it up, what to spend it on. It's one thing for you to extend your hand to give all you can spare, quite another for your family to stick out theirs, expecting to take. "Don't you ever ask me to lend you some money again in this world," you snapped last October. "If you do I won't send it to you."

There's a nervous excitement rippling through the regiment as you wait for the command to get going, and it's not just shivers from the twelve-degree air. Today is not like last April—back then, you were all ready to march, loaded up with three days' rations, but nothing happened. You were all still fairly green, anyhow. Today, though—today is serious.

You feel like you're in good hands with the colonel up there—Colonel Edwin P. Davis. Colonel Davis saw action in the Battle of the Seven Days, right before you joined up. And even if he's not exactly been in a rush to get the rest of you a taste of battle, you can't help but look up to him—so much that you wish you'd thought of "Edwin" before you started going by "Lyons."

Army food and Army drills have made you fat as a hog and tough as a bear. You've got the company and battalion drills down pat—regular speed or double-quick, it doesn't matter. In Alexandria, it was guard one day and drill the next—loading and firing blank cartridges over the shoulders of the men in front of you, as the soldiers in the row behind did the same. When the draft heated up last summer and it looked like there might be riots, the 153rd got moved to Washington, D.C.

Here on Capitol Hill, the 153rd has guarded Carroll Prison, the B&O railroad depot, and City Hall, plus the camp itself. You've seen Negroes get drafted just like white—that's a big change, even just since you joined up.

Some of the others get all het up over the reasons for fighting this war, but you haven't had much to say about it. All the same, you've been hoping to see some real action—at least, that's what you've told your parents, and isn't that the manly thing to say?

The longer the war lasts, the longer you get to enjoy living this way. Too often, though, there's been nothing to do—not what some expect from life in a wartime army, but it's true. And when there's nothing to do, the more time folks have to stick their noses into somebody else's affairs—and the greater the risk that someone will stumble onto your secret and try to send you home.

It would be at their peril, you believe. "I can take care of my Self and I know my business," you wrote your folks. "I will Dress as I am a mind to . . . and if they don't let me Alone they will be sorry for it."

That brings to mind something you haven't written to your family about, something that's none of their concern nor anybody else's: how you've managed to keep secret that you're a woman. In such close quarters as those enjoyed by members of the Union Army, it can be a bit challenging to find the privacy you need day to day and month to month, but not so much as folks might think. The doctor's examination you got when you joined up was hardly worthy of the name, and not even your bout with the measles a year ago brought you much attention.

It's something of an odd position you're in. In a way, Rosetta, you can be yourself in the Army, even if that self wears britches and goes by the name of Private Wakeman. You fit in: You can bluster and grumble as well as the rest of them—about those Copperhead Democrats trying to quit the war before you've won it, and about officer pay, and how good you are with an Enfield rifle, and of course about the long odds those rebels would face should they choose to tangle with you. You use up your share of tobacco too.

But the soldiers who see you every day, you can't let them truly *know* you, not even a little. And the people who know you—your family—they can't see you, other than in the black-and-white likeness you sent home, with you in your Army coat and cap, standing as stiff as the rifle in your right arm and looking straight ahead. "Do you think I look better than I did when I was to home?" you asked in the letter you sent along with it. Just how did you expect them to answer?

Here's a question for you, though: Who are you going to be when this war is over, and if you're around to see that day, God willing? You're earning a man's wage now, and you expect to earn a man's wage when you get out—for your family's debts, and for yourself. It's hard to see yourself ever getting to have that independent life if you don't stick it out now, if you don't put up with the risk that there might be a rebel's bullet or cannonball out there with your name on it.

If there is one, you won't be seeing it soon. Assuming you don't freeze to death while waiting, you'll set out any moment now, but you're not about to march right into battle. For now, you're just heading a few miles down the road. All you've heard is that you're getting on the boat in Alexandria, getting off in New Orleans, and heading toward Texas.

A little bit ago, you took pen in hand to tell your family as much. When that was done, what else was there to say? "I bid you all good-by," you wrote. "Don't never expect to see you again."

And below that, you signed, "Edwin R. Wakeman."

Forward, march.

WHAT HAPPENED NEXT?

SARAH ROSETTA WAKEMAN marched with the 153rd from Franklin, Louisiana, and battled Confederate troops at Pleasant Hill and Monett's Bluff during the Red River Campaign of spring 1864. "I was under fire about four hours and laid on the field of battle all night," she wrote after her first engagement. Like many in her unit, Wakeman soon developed acute diarrhea. As it did to tens of thousands of soldiers on both sides, the ailment killed her: She died in a New Orleans hospital on June 19. Of the hundreds of women who posed as men in order to fight in the Civil War, Wakeman is the only one whose letters home are known to have survived.

HITLER·YOUTH?
SOLOMON PEREL

LATE JUNE 1941

NEAR MINSK, BELARUS

Your name is Solomon Perel. You're a short, skinny, sixteen-year-old Jew, and you've just been captured by the Nazis. It's all you can do not to piss yourself.

They've nabbed you and a bunch of other refugees, just a few days into Germany's invasion of the Soviet Union. Now they've lined you all up in a field as they decide what to do with each of you.

Most of you are Jewish—that's why you were on the run in the first place—so the Nazis don't have to think too hard about it. They take groups of refugees ahead of you off into the woods. From the forest come the sounds of shovels and machine guns, shovels and machine guns.

Your wait stretches into hours. That's plenty of time to consider the papers in your pocket, the ones identifying you not only as a Jew but also as a Communist—a Nazi target twice over.

If you run, you'll be killed for sure. And so, hoping no one will notice amid the smoke and bombs and hum of German planes, you gouge a hole in the earth with the heel of your shoe. You drop those incriminating papers into the hole and sweep the dirt on top of them. The Germans are sticklers for proper documentation, but now you have none. It's almost as if you have no identity at all.

Your turn. A soldier orders you to put your trembling hands above your head. He frisks you and asks: "Are you a Jew?"

Calmly, somehow, you reply: "I'm not a Jew."

You tell him that you're a *Volksdeutscher*—a person with German ancestors but not German citizenship. You're not the first in line to lie. If this soldier doubts you—like he did the others—he'll pull down your pants, see that you've been circumcised, and send you off to the forest.

But he doesn't. God knows why, but he believes you.

"Sir," he proudly tells his sergeant, "we found a young German among this human garbage." What a discovery!

How lucky for him.

1941–1942
ON THE EASTERN FRONT

An anti-tank unit of the 12th Panzer Division takes you in. They give you a meal and a too-big uniform. In return you give them a made-up name: "Josef Perjell."

You give them a story to match: You're Lithuanian, and you've been an orphan your whole life. Your papers were destroyed in a German bombing. And that's that.

Here's your real story:

Your parents, brothers, and sister are Polish, but you—the youngest—were born and raised in the German town of Peine. You grew up hearing Adolf Hitler call your people bloodsuckers and parasites. His Stormtroopers wrote "Don't buy from Jews!" on the windows of your father's shoe store. Swastikas appeared everywhere. The Nazis kicked you out of school when you were ten. Your family went back to Poland.

Three years later, the German army invaded. You watched soldiers beat Jews in the streets of Lodz. Every week, the occupiers clamped down harder, and the Führer's bluster about extermination and annihilation couldn't just be waved away. "You *must* stay alive," your mother pleaded, and your parents sent you farther east, into Belarus. On that rugged December journey, you wore your Bar Mitzvah suit. For a year and a half, you lived in an orphanage. You learned Russian and joined the Communist Party.

Now you're hiding among the army you fled, translating the interrogations of Russian prisoners. Your sympathies are with the Russians, of course, but you can't let those feelings show. You learn to think one thing but say another. You have a role to play, and your life depends on playing it flawlessly.

To the soldiers in your unit, you're sort of a cross between a little brother, a mascot, and a good luck charm. They watch over you so closely that there's no way you can escape.

One officer, Heinz, watches you more closely than the others. One night, you're bathing in an abandoned house, and you think you're alone—until Heinz sneaks up from behind and grabs you. Slipping free from his clinch, you turn to face him. He looks down, and he *sees*.

Thwarted, embarrassed, and now very, very puzzled, he says nothing for several moments. Finally, he asks, "Are you Jewish?"

The answer is obvious, and you have never felt so vulnerable. "Don't kill me!" you beg.

Will he turn you in? What price will you pay for his silence? Or, seeing as the Third Reich cares no more for homosexuals than it does for Jews, will you each hold the other in check—your knowledge of his secret vs. his knowledge of yours?

"Don't cry," he says. "You know, there *is* another Germany."

Heinz keeps your secret, no strings attached. You come to understand that German soldiers aren't necessarily actual *Nazis*. Some aren't fighting because they share Hitler's hatred, they're fighting because they were told to fight. A few are pretty cynical about the war. You still fear them—never for a moment are you lulled into thinking you'd be safe among them as Solomon instead of Josef—but you can't help but like them. They're your card-playing, beer-drinking buddies—genuine pals. And when Heinz gets hit during a Russian attack, you crawl out from under the tank where he had pulled you to safety just moments before. You hold him as he bleeds to death.

Not long after, the powers that be decide you're too young to be on the front lines of the war. No person your age should be subjected to such a horrible thing. You're ordered back to Germany.

1942–1944
BRUNSWICK, GERMANY

They send "Josef Perjell" to a boarding school for the Hitler Youth. They want to mold their splendid *Volksdeutscher* find from the Eastern Front into a grade-A Nazi. Back with your unit, you were among a bunch of guys who were just doing their jobs. Here, you're surrounded by Nazi true believers armed with daggers inscribed "Blood and Honor." And you're supposed to feel safer?

It gets worse. The school is in Brunswick, not even twenty miles from your hometown of Peine. What if someone recognizes you as that little Jewish boy who left seven years ago?

That's not the only thing you're afraid of. What if you talk in your sleep, speaking Yiddish or saying something else revealing? Each morning, the first thing you do is check your roommate's expression for signs that you've betrayed yourself in the night. There's also your circumcision. You wear your underwear in the shower, but you worry that your schoolmates will suspect you of something more than mere modesty.

You hide your fears behind stiff-armed Nazi salutes and greetings of "Heil Hitler!" You've been disqualified from potential membership in the Führer's all-powerful S.S.—at five two, you're too short, and you have black hair instead of Aryan blond. But in your swastika-adorned uniform, you look like your fellow students, and you act like they do. They think they're invincible, destined to rule the world, and their confidence is intoxicating. You can't help but feel it too.

At the same time, you ache for your family. You long to simply be around other Jews. For all you know, you're the only one left in Germany. And beyond Germany—who knows? You've read of a plan to send all of Europe's Jews to the African island of Madagascar.

It's impossible for you to see such a scheme or anything else—any idea, any person, any situation—just one way. There's the point of view you have to have, no matter how much you despise it, so that you'll act the way a Hitler Youth is supposed to act. And then there's the way you really feel: tormented. Torn. Enveloped in layers of hatred: of Solomon for being Jewish, of Josef Perjell for hating Solomon, and of Solomon Perel for being Josef.

You ping-pong between being alarmingly cocky that your deception will last and swimming in anxiety that you'll be found out. Your schoolmates' dinnertime sing-alongs don't help: "We'll be even better off once Jewish blood spurts from our knives," goes one song. For your studies, you read and reread Hitler's rants against Jews. In the classroom you force a smile as you recite the themes.

The teacher in your class on racial theory, Borgdorf, rattles off stereotypical physical traits of Jews. You grow certain that you resemble this one, and that one, and another one too, and that it's only a matter of time before everyone notices.

One day, Borgdorf calls you to the front of the room. You tremble as you walk up the aisle.

"Class, take a look at Josef," he says.

Oh, God.

But then:

"He is a typical descendant of the Eastern Baltic race."

In other words, an Aryan, like the rest of them.

Fools.

Near the school, there's a pastry shop with a sign on the door reading "No dogs or Jews allowed"—as if there were any Jews left in Brunswick. You go inside every time you pass by. This little bit of defiance helps relieve a little bit of the pressure you feel building up inside you.

There's nobody you can tell the truth to—nobody you feel you can trust. Not even Leni, the local girl you've begun dating. She's in the BDM—Hitler Youth for girls. Members of both groups are encouraged to report their parents for opposing the Nazis. There's no reason to think she'd protect you.

When you go to see Leni one day, she's not at home, but her mother invites you in. There's something on her mind.

After a long silence, Mrs. Latsch asks, "Are you really German?"

Caught off guard, you tell the truth. "Please don't report me," you whisper.

You lucked out. Little things about Josef Perjell's life's story just didn't add up for Mrs. Latsch, but you picked the right person to be careless with. She kisses you on the forehead and tells you that your secret is safe—but she makes you swear not to tell Leni. She doesn't trust her daughter any more than you do.

DECEMBER 1943
LODZ, POLAND

You hear your classmates making plans to go home to their families for the holidays, and you decide you should be able to do the same. You'll need the school to provide a travel permit, train tickets, food ration cards, and some cash.

"I would like to go on vacation," you tell the administrators.

"Oh, and where would you like to go?" one of them asks in surprise, knowing that you're an orphan.

"To Lodz," you say. "I want to settle some affairs."

What you want is to find your parents and to . . . what? What is your plan, exactly? When you get to the walled ghetto your parents wrote to you about when you were in the orphanage, what will you do? What will you do if you find your parents? And what if you don't? What then?

Your first morning in Lodz, you climb onto a street-car marked "For Germans Only." Your black uniform shows that you are a Hitler Youth—who could question you? You travel past streets that the Nazis have renamed since you left, and so you almost miss the stop that you once knew as Freedom Square.

You walk past a heap of rubble—torn-down houses, the better to isolate the ghetto from the rest of the city. You scale one of those piles of debris and look down, beyond the barbed wire, into the ghetto. For the first time in years, you see other Jews.

They're gray-skinned, shabbily dressed, and wasting away in an urban prison. This is what your disguise has shielded you from. This is what your parents have endured—if they have survived at all.

You approach the gate, only to be stopped by a *Volksdeutscher* guard. "You must have lost your way," he tells you, careful not to offend a Hitler Youth and real German. "Only Jews live here. You are not allowed here." Diseases, you know.

The only way into the ghetto is through it, on a nonstop streetcar locked up tight to keep any Jews from climbing on board to escape. You get on, standing behind the driver. No other passengers seem to notice the dreadful scene outside the windows, but you can't look away.

And there it is—the apartment house at 18 Franciszkan'ska, the address where you sent your letters years ago. You stare at the decrepit dwelling as if the power of your own yearning could draw Mama and Papa outside to watch the passing streetcar. But there is no sign of them. Where *are* they? In silence, you pass through to the other side of the ghetto.

During your days in Lodz, you take the streetcar back and forth, back and forth, as often as you think you can get away with without raising suspicions. But you never see your parents—not at the apartment house, not on the footbridges you pass beneath, not among the weary souls trudging along with bundles of scrap wood. Why don't you try to slip into the ghetto on foot and try to find them? Because you don't need to sneak inside in order to hear Mama's words: "You *must* stay alive."

APRIL 1945
ON THE WESTERN FRONT

Last October, British bombers did their best to destroy Brunswick. With the Allies closing in, you were sent to the front and taught how to use an anti-tank rocket launcher. Your commanders thought you'd use it to defend the Fatherland. You knew you'd do no such thing. In your hands, that weapon was just a prop for a part you'd play while waiting for the good guys to arrive.

They come into your camp in the earliest hours of

your twentieth birthday, on April 21. You're awoken with a whack from a rifle butt. "Up against the wall, Nazis!" the Americans bellow. If these guys are your liberators, they sure don't know it. And for some reason, you can't bring yourself to tell them.

They take your weapons, confiscate your camera, and strip you of all your Nazi badges and emblems. And then, into a land turned upside down, they set your unit free. But freedom for you is not a gate, a quick passage from one state to another. Rather, it's a long tunnel. You need time for your eyes to adjust to the light. It finally happens when you see a man in a prisoner's uniform, shaven-headed and starving and with the word "Jew" on his shirt.

A Jew, free, in Germany. At last.

"Excuse me, sir," you begin. "Are you really Jewish?" You ask this while still dressed in your Hitler Youth uniform. The man does not reply. To be called "sir" by a Hitler Youth must seem as unreal to him as his very presence does to you. He cannot imagine what will happen next.

You wrap your arms around this stranger. You hug him. "I'm a Jew too," you whisper. "My name is Solomon Perel."

WHAT HAPPENED NEXT?

SOLOMON PEREL'S brothers also survived the war, but their sister and parents did not. Perel moved to Israel in 1948 and later opened a zipper factory. After undergoing heart surgery when he was in his fifties, he began writing down his story of wartime survival. His book, *Europa, Europa*, was published in 1990, and it began a second career for him as a lecturer about the toll of his experiences as Josef Perjell. "I still hate him," he said of Josef Perjell fifty years later, "but I still love him. He saved my life."

The Education of Little Tree
A true story

CHEROKEE AUTHOR?
FORREST CARTER

Well, Forrest, as authors of best-selling books for children go, you sure are extraordinary.

For one thing, before *The Education of Little Tree* came along, you were best known for writing a novel that became a violent Clint Eastwood Western.

For another, you've been dead twelve years.

Of course, there's something else too—but we'll get to that in a minute.

Today, *Little Tree* is number one on the best seller list for paperback nonfiction. Your Depression-era tale of life with your Cherokee grandparents in the Tennessee hills—"A True Story," says the cover—has become a book that people love to tell other readers about, like they're letting them in on a secret.

Maybe they're reacting to your neat trick of telling your story from a five-year-old's perspective—matter-of-fact, sweetly naive, yet somehow wise beyond his years. It makes the heartbreaking parts all the more tender and the funny parts all the more laugh-out-loud.

And though *The Education of Little Tree* is occasionally risqué—what with all the talk of moonshine and fornication—teachers in middle schools and high schools have taken to sharing your book with their students. They say it's one that these kids really need to read.

That audience may not be one that you had in mind when you wrote the book. But honestly, who could have predicted any of this?

As an author, you seemed to come from out of nowhere around 1973, a middle-aged cowboy drifter with no yarn-spinning past other than the stretch you said you'd to have spent as Storyteller in Council to the Cherokee Nations. You were peddling a self-published novel about Josey Wales, a pro-Confederate guerrilla after the Civil War. That's not the sort of thing that big New York City publishers were knocking each other over to get their hands on, but your tale of Wales's quest for a new life and identity caught the eye of one. And your exotic background and entertainingly rough-around-the-edges personality surely helped seal the deal.

They made the rare decision to republish that shoot-'em-up page-turner themselves, and *The Rebel Outlaw:*

Josey Wales got made into that Clint Eastwood movie in '76. Along the way, you found your cowboy-hatted, newly mustachioed self on TV in front of millions of viewers one morning, talking with Barbara Walters on the *Today* show.

You kept working, turning out another Josey Wales book, and one about Geronimo, and *The Education of Little Tree*. You also generated your share of commotion, especially when you had too much to drink and let loose with eyebrow-raising comments about blacks and Jews.

Eventually, you got drunk and out of hand one time too many, and a fistfight left you dead. Just half a dozen years after becoming an author, it was all over for you. And as so often happens in publishing, *The Education of Little Tree* faded away too. The publisher figured that pretty much everyone who was ever going to read your story had already bought a copy, so they stopped printing new ones.

But then something else happened that almost never does: *Little Tree*'s editor found a new publisher for it—in New Mexico, of all places. The book came back into print, and you, in a sense, came back from the dead. It was only the beginning of an incredible new story—a story about a story.

Readers who discovered *The Education of Little Tree* on its second time around couldn't stop talking about it. However many copies of *Little Tree* were sold one year, twice as many were sold the year after that. Booksellers, especially, loved to connect customers with this beautiful little book—so spiritual, and funny—about a Native American boy and his grandparents. Many readers saw an environmental message as the young Cherokee learns of "The Way" and "Mon-o-lah, the Earth mother" from his nature-loving Granma and Granpa. What a wonderful multicultural book to share with students.

Little Tree kept striking a chord with readers who wouldn't know a Cherokee from a Cheyenne. Sales doubled again and again, which led to newspaper and magazine articles about the phenomenon. It all just added to the warm feeling folks got from the book itself. Those articles led to more sales, which led to more publicity, which led to . . .

This.

This article, right here, in today's *New York Times*. "*The Education of Little Tree*," it says, "is a hoax." It also says that—well, you don't need to be told what all it says, because it's your life it's talking about. Your actual life, Ace.

But for all those readers who never heard of Asa Earl Carter, the article fills them in. On his—your—decades-long career as a fiery Alabama racist. On your membership in the Ku Klux Klan. On your talent for whipping bigots into a frenzy, and for taking matters into your own vicious hands on occasion.

Of course, the article brings up the most famous words you ever wrote—as a speechwriter for Alabama governor George Wallace. Better known than any you ever put in the mouths of Josey Wales or Little Tree, they were proclaimed by the governor on the statehouse steps in 1963: "Segregation now . . . segregation tomorrow . . . segregation forever!"

Those words were a signal to the world that men like you weren't about to let the non-white, non-Christian people of the South get on an equal footing. An unrepentant decade later, you disappeared without comment on those sentiments—with neither affirmation nor apology. But anyone looking for clues to your frame of mind could be excused for seeing one in the new name you adopted: Forrest, after Confederate general and Klansman Nathan Bedford Forrest.

In the character of Josey Wales, you showed a certain flair for romanticizing the lost cause of the Confederacy while depicting the North's endless persecution of Southerners. If that was simply the point of view of a literary character, well, he didn't represent much of an artistic stretch for you.

Little Tree, though—Little Tree was something different. You may have stuffed *The Education of Little Tree* with generous amounts of hooey—really: "Mon-o-lah"?—and the federal government didn't come off any better than it did in *Rebel Outlaw*. But at the heart of *The Education of Little Tree* you placed a vivid, sympathetic character far removed from your legacy as Ace Carter. That little-boy version of your "Forrest Carter" creation made it clear that you had grown as a writer.

Had you grown as a person, though? That's the question confronting newspaper readers today. But it's not the first time that question's been asked, now is it? And it's not the first time it will go unanswered.

When an Alabama newspaperman connected your pen name with your true identity fifteen years ago— right after the Josey Wales movie came out—it was mildly denied but otherwise met with silence. Readers forgot about it, or ignored it, or never noticed it in the first place. With *The Education of Little Tree* a best seller, that's not likely to happen again.

But if there's one thing that experience taught you about readers in particular and the public in general, it's this: Just because they've been shown the truth doesn't mean they'll stop buying your story.

WHAT HAPPENED NEXT?

IN THE WEEKS after *The New York Times* revealed Forrest Carter's true identity, Carter's widow acknowledged that her husband and Ace Carter were the same man. Though the publisher removed "A True Story" from the book's cover and reclassified it as fiction, *The Education of Little Tree* remained a best seller, retained many supporters, and was made into a movie. In 2007, the debate over whether the author's background diminishes the book was revived when the title was found on—and removed from—a list of recommended reading on the website of TV host Oprah Winfrey. It has sold more than 1.5 million copies.

KIDNAPPED PRINCESS?
PRINCESS CARABOO

SUNDAY, JUNE 8, 1817

BATH, ENGLAND

You are a fibber. A confabulator. Mary Baker, you're a liar. You make up stories about yourself as easily as other people make their beds. And you're rarely without an audience eager to be fooled.

You certainly were in your element last night—the Saturday crowd at the Pack Horse Inn was made for stringing along. Running off from Bristol had made you thirsty, but not so thirsty that you broke character. As the exotic Princess Caraboo, you drew a picture of a tree. Eventually someone figured out that it was supposed to be a tea tree, and you received a cupful.

This morning, you're back at it. You're having breakfast with the Pack Horse's landlady—who believes that *she's* having breakfast with a mysterious foreigner—when a gentleman walks into the room.

Oh, no.

Not him!

It's Dr. Wilkinson. He knows everything about Princess Caraboo—and though that means, of course, that he actually knows nothing, your relief over being gone from Bristol disappears.

How did he know you were here? Did you let down your guard last night? Did you slip up and stray too far from the persona you've perfected these past two months? Does he suspect anything?

You begin to sob, covering your face with a handkerchief. But you pull yourself together and lower the handkerchief, and you discover that nothing between you and him seems to have changed. If Dr. Wilkinson has interpreted your tears as a sign of guilt—if he doubts that you are, indeed, Princess Caraboo from the island of Javasu—he doesn't let on.

Still, you've got to get out of here.

You go outside and begin making your way to the middle of Bath.

Dr. Wilkinson has blown things all out of proportion. Thanks to him, what began for you as a lark—donning a turban and pretending not to speak English—has become news as far off as London and Edinburgh.

But let's be fair. Yes, Dr. Wilkinson may have been

unusually enchanted by the identity you've created. But many people have been intrigued by it, and you've certainly done nothing to discourage that.

In fact, you've let them help invent that identity. Princess Caraboo is as much their creation as yours.

She began so simply. You arrived in Almondsbury, just outside Bristol, on April 3—at loose ends, on foot, and practically empty-handed. You wore your black shawl on your head, a black dress, black stockings, and leather shoes—nothing exotic.

But no matter how many languages the local folks tried, you seemed not to understand them, and you addressed them in a tongue that none of them recognized. You'd had practice at that—you and your little sister used to lie in bed for hours jabbering back and forth in a lingo no one else could comprehend.

Late in the evening, Elizabeth Worrall, the wife of the town clerk, arranged for you to have a private room and a meal at a local inn. On a wall there you saw a picture of a pineapple, and you indicated that it grew in your homeland. The innkeeper made you some tea, and before you drank it you covered your eyes and uttered something that sounded like a prayer. When the cup was refilled, you refused to drink from it until you had washed the cup yourself and repeated the prayer ritual.

They were captivated. You were just getting started.

Hoping to divine your origins, the next morning

the vicar brought books with geographic prints and engravings. You couldn't read English—or so he believed—but he thought you might see something you recognized. For you, this was on-the-spot research into the role you were playing. You pointed out prints of China, indicating that you had been brought from there on a ship.

Mrs. Worrall took you home with her. Whatever language she thought you might be speaking, she was determined to break through to you. She wrote her own name, spoke it, repeated it, and handed you her pen. You shook your head and pointed at yourself. "Caraboo," you said. "Caraboo."

"Caraboo?" Well, why not?

Mrs. Worrall took you on a tour of the house, and when you saw Chinese figures on the furniture, you reacted as if they were familiar to you. You began piling quirk on top of quirk. At dinner, you appeared disgusted by the notion of eating meat, and you refused all beverages other than water. Never mind the rum and steak you'd shared just two days earlier with that dull young fellow you'd met while traveling (and gladly ditched soon after).

You attracted plenty of visitors who tried to figure out who you were and where you came from—but who evidently gave no thought to what a person from Asia might actually look like. One of them pretended to understand your language—a mixture of dialects from the Sumatran coast and nearby islands, he explained. Through that "understanding," he came away with the story that you were an important person on your island home, one who had been kidnapped and then somehow became free in England.

Sumatra? A person of importance? Kidnapped? A houseguest that intriguing could expect to stay on the Worrall estate for a while.

And so you did—and what a show you put on! You would kneel by the pond, pray in the bushes, wear flowers and feathers in your hair, and beat a gong and tambourine in the garden. You climbed trees, swam na-ked, shot arrows while running about, and rowed Mrs. Worrall around the pond.

Mrs. Worrall's friends, enchanted, came with ob-jects for you to examine and secondhand stories of Asia to share with each other. Before them, you mugged, danced, gesticulated—and *paid attention*. Once they accepted that you could not speak English, they would say anything in front of you, all the time feeding you the material you needed to further your masquerade.

That dagger, for example. One dedicated visitor brought an Asian dagger, explaining to the other visi-tors how the natives used poison on the tip. Soon after, you just happened to demonstrate, rubbing juice from the leaves of a houseplant onto the blade, poking yourself with the tip, and then pretending to faint from the toxins.

And all those books—what would you have done without them? Those the vicar had brought were just the beginning. No one suspected that you could actually make sense of the words while you perused the pictures.

One guest brought a big book about Java, and your response was clear. This, you wanted them to understand, was your home.

When another book included examples of Sumatran dialects, you seized on them—these, you wanted them to know, formed the tongue you spoke. And with a little inspiration from a volume depicting written languages from around the globe—Arabic and Persic, Sanskrit and Greek, Chinese and Malay—you produced spirals and loops and diamonds and dots from your own language.

You took apart the information provided by those visitors, and then you put it back together in a way different enough and sufficiently exotic for your listeners to accept as the way things were in your homeland.

What's more, you were consistent. "Lazor" always meant "ladies," "manjintoo" always meant "gentlemen," "rampue" always meant "pigeon," and so forth. You always greeted visitors with the palm of your hand placed against your temple—on the left for women, on the right for men. And after you got such a reaction with a morning escapade to the rooftop—where you chanted to "Alla Tallah," the name for God that you spotted on page 316 of *Pantographia*—you made sure you returned to the roof each Tuesday.

Above all, you flattered those who came to gawk at you. Or, rather, you gave them the opportunity to flatter themselves by showing how much they knew (or imagined they did) about exotic topics and showing how cultured the titles on their bookshelves were. They may have been making fools of themselves, but they sure *felt* smarter.

At last, this Sunday morning in Bath, you have arrived at the Circus, this great circular plaza in the middle of town. For now, you're alone, but can Dr. Wilkinson be far behind? As you stroll about, never far from your mind is the story you concocted with the unwitting collaboration of the Worralls' bluestocking guests—the story of how Princess Caraboo got to England in the first place.

It involved not only a kidnapping but also deadly hand-to-hand combat. And two sets of pirates. And surgery performed on the back of your neck before you finally jumped overboard and swam onto the shores of England.

You do have a scar at the base of your skull. And in fact, you did obtain that scar in the midst of an ordeal.

It's just that your actual ordeal did not resemble in the slightest the one that you shared with the folks in Almondsbury.

You were born Mary Ann Willcocks twenty-six years ago in Witheridge, Devonshire. A cobbler's daughter, you were poor, and poorly educated. After a falling-out with your family, you left home without a penny or a change of clothes.

Eventually, as you neared London, begging along the way and sleeping in haylofts when you had to, you got sick and were admitted to a hospital. You were there for months, feverish and delirious. To try to set you right, they made an incision on the back of your neck, covering it with a warm cup to draw out your bad blood.

When they released you, you stayed in London, working for the Matthews family and caring for their children. Mrs. Matthews and her daughter gave you informal lessons in writing and reading. You also gained some attention from the Matthewses by making the extraordinary claim—inspired by the fasting of the Jewish man next door?—that you sometimes went several days without eating.

For six months after that, you lived at the Magdalen Hospital, a home for repentant prostitutes. You made up a background for yourself in order to get in, starting with the claim that you were an orphan whose father died when you were a newborn.

A year later, in a London bookstore, you met a man called Baker. But after traveling around together for a few months—long enough for you to get pregnant—he gave you the slip. You told different people different made-up stories about who the father was.

While pregnant, you worked at the Crab Tree pub. During your six months there, you called yourself Hannah, said your husband was dead, and told stories so outrageous that they delighted many a soul but fooled none of them. You gave birth to a son last year and left him at the foundling hospital—though you lived nearby and visited your baby each Monday.

You became a servant for the Starling family—alternately entertaining and scaring the daylights out of their children with your stories—near the end of October. Right around that time, your son died. The next month, the Starlings dismissed you for setting fire to two beds in one week.

It was five months later that Princess Caraboo appeared in Bristol. You had picked back up on your old pastime of begging, and doing so in a made-up tongue. You also found a begging partner—your roommate at a boarding house—and together you came up with the idea to make yourself more intriguing by wearing your black shawl as a turban.

Combined with your lingo, it did the trick, and you decided to try your luck alone in the countryside around Bristol. You could don and shed your exotic-foreigner persona at will—but that was about to change. You were about to take up that role around the clock before an endless audience of visitor after visitor.

Among them has been Dr. Wilkinson. He examined your scar and confirmed that it certainly had not been made by any Englishman or European. In the first days of June, his accounts of his meeting with you began to be published in newspapers all over England, complete with a gushing and detailed description of you:

> . . . a sweet smile; her mouth rather large; her teeth beautifully white and regular; her lips a little prominent and full, under lip rather projecting; her chin small and round . . . She appears to be about 25 years of age; her manners are extremely graceful, her countenance surprisingly fascinating . . .

You were flattered, of course. But it's one thing to fool a family or a single community, and quite another to be put on stage before an entire nation. With that mounting, suffocating pressure, is it any wonder that you bolted to Bath? You left behind all the trinkets and objects you'd been given to examine, no matter their worth. You covered the two dozen miles by foot and by cart, and here you are.

And there he is. Dr. Wilkinson has caught up with you here at the Circus. Like a persistent hound—a puppy, really—he's following you as you stroll around the railed garden in the middle.

Well, he's not following *you*—he's following Princess Caraboo.

MONDAY, JUNE 9, 1817
ALMONDSBURY, ENGLAND

It's the next morning, and you're back at the Worralls'.

After Dr. Wilkinson accompanied you back to the gathering crowd at the Pack Horse, two women suggested to him that their home would offer you more privacy. Your new hosts had you carried there in a sedan chair. When Mrs. Worrall caught up with you—Dr. Wilkinson must have sent word to her—you were entertaining a more reasonably sized crowd in their drawing room.

As you wordlessly discoursed in all things Caraboo, these people knelt before you, wanted to touch you, drove you dangerously close to a fit of laughter that would have given yourself away. At the sight of Mrs.

Worrall, however, you were the one falling to your knees, begging forgiveness for running away.

She forgave you. You managed to keep up the charade for another day. But as your fame spreads, in person and through the newspapers, how much longer can it be before someone pieces "Princess Caraboo" together with the person you were before the day you wandered into Almondsbury? For all the kindness she has shown, doesn't Mrs. Worrall deserve to be the first to know the truth?

You approach Mrs. Worrall's dressing room. She invites you in, and you lock the door behind you. And you tell her . . .

Nothing.

You just can't.

Not while you still have a choice.

WHAT HAPPENED NEXT?

MARY BAKER HAD only one more day as "Princess Caraboo" before testimony from her former Bristol landlady and the dull young man she'd traveled with exposed her as a fraud. She cooperated—mostly—with an investigation by rightfully skeptical journalist John Matthew Gutch, who published a full account of her life that August. By then she'd left for a short-lived, unsuccessful bid for American fame. Back in England, she made her living selling leeches to hospitals until she died in 1864.

SLAVE OWNER?
ELLEN CRAFT

FRIDAY, DECEMBER 22, 1848
CHARLESTON, SOUTH CAROLINA

At twenty-two, you cannot read or write.

A week ago in Macon, Georgia, before this plan came into the heads of you and your husband and consumed you like fever, that did not matter. Of course you couldn't read or write, Ellen—no matter how light-skinned, you were a slave. Anyone who taught you to put pen to paper or make out the words on a page would have been breaking the law. Ellen Craft could not read or write, and that was that. The same went for your William.

But here near the wharf in Charleston, your illiteracy is another matter entirely. What is expected of you could not be more different than it was a week ago. In the eyes of those around you, you are not a seamstress or a slave. You are not even a Negro, not even a woman at all.

You are "Mr. Johnson"—a Southern gentleman. Which is to say, a *white* Southern gentleman. And a white Southern gentleman who cannot read or write would stick out like a field slave who cannot find the opening of a cotton sack.

Needless to say, you and your accompanying "slave"—William—do not wish to stick out. At least, not in that way. That's why the plan the two of you cooked up includes a thorough disguise. Along with your trousers, top hat, green spectacles, and handkerchief tied beneath your apparently aching jaw, you're sporting a sling for your poor, rheumatic writing arm.

Such a young man, and in such sad shape—not much more than an invalid, really. How fortunate that William is here to attend to you, to assist you on your thousand-mile journey to seek help for your rheumatism from your physician uncle in Philadelphia, a city that just happens to be located in the free state of Pennsylvania.

Your masquerade has held up this past day and a half, from Macon to Savannah by train, and then by steamboat to Charleston. Now you just need to get your steamer tickets for the Charleston-to-Philadelphia leg, and you'll be out of the South—and out of slavery—for good.

But there is a hitch in your plan: Now that winter is here, you learn, the steamboat doesn't run that direct route. You'll need to follow a patchwork path by steamer and rail. Fine—you wouldn't have gotten this far if you weren't able to adapt. You hand over the fare, and the ticket man hands over the tickets.

Situations such as this pose one particular danger, but you wouldn't have put your right arm in this sling if the thought hadn't already occurred to you: Where along the way might you be expected to sign your name?

And the answer is: Here.

Now.

You pay your one-dollar duty on your piece of human property, but now you need to sign the registry stating that you are taking your slave to the North. Indicating your weakened arm, you ask the customs officer if he would be so kind as to sign your name for you. He reacts as if he's been burned.

He rises and shakes his head and jams his hands down into his pockets. "I shan't do it," he insists.

Everybody knows what becomes of slaves once they've seen life up North—it spoils them, and even if they don't escape, even if they do return home, they poison other slaves' minds with Northern nonsense about freedom. And this customs man certainly cannot condone that.

He's causing a scene in the middle of the day, and that's the last thing you need. You aren't yet 300 miles from Macon—near enough that reward-seekers might already be on the lookout for you and William in this very office. Any disturbance raises the risk of getting caught, and surely the first thing they would do is separate you from your coconspirator—forever. How can you resolve this situation and quiet things down without abandoning your disguise of a man just barely hanging on?

A young Southern military man comes to your rescue. You met this fellow yesterday, traveled with him again this morning, and aren't likely ever to forget him. Witnessing your civil treatment of William, this military fellow lectured you about the need to keep a slave in his place, to "storm at him like thunder, and make him tremble like a leaf." And at least in his current drunken state, your receipt of his advice qualifies you as one of his best friends.

"I know his kin like a book," he tells the customs man. The steamboat captain overhears, and the word of this military man and yourself—two distinguished white men—is good enough for him. He accepts that this Mr. Johnson is indeed the owner of this slave.

Soon, you and William are on board.

Later, before you get off the boat in Wilmington, you cross the captain's path again, and he recalls the scene back at the customs office.

"They make it a rule to be very strict at Charleston," he explains. "If they were not very careful, any damned abolitionist might take off a lot of valuable niggers."

"I suppose so," you reply.

SATURDAY, DECEMBER 23, 1848
CHESTER, VIRGINIA

They think you're asleep.

This older man and his daughters boarded the train just south of here, in Petersburg. While William rides elsewhere with other Negroes, these kind travelers have joined you in the private compartment at the end of this carriage. They take pity on you. There are two couches, and they help you get situated on one of them. The young ladies offer their shawls to serve as your pillow.

"Papa, he seems to be a very nice young gentleman," one of them says.

"Oh, dear me," says the other, "I never felt so much for a gentleman in my life."

You keep your reaction to yourself. You know how quickly their kindness would vanish if they discovered how different you are from the person you appear to be.

And yet . . .

The color of your skin is genuine. There was no need to lighten it for your journey. In the eyes of your owners, it is your Negro blood that dictates your fate.

But to these travelers who do not know your true story, it is your color that determines who you are.

And that color is white.

In some ways, it has been a blessing—your current bid for freedom depends on it, and as the lives of human chattel go, your light skin has made yours relatively privileged. Even your manner of speech indicates a life spent in the shade of the house rather than in the heat of the fields. But your whiteness has caused you pain too. When you were eleven years old, it got you torn apart from your mother, Maria.

That separation was a punishment for your undeniable resemblance to your mother's master, James P. Smith. Your familiar features and fair skin—lighter even than Maria's—were an ever-present reminder of things Mrs. Smith did not wish to remember: The master's indulgence. Her own humiliation. Your mother's rape.

Mrs. Smith's cruelty to you became routine. When her daughter was married, Mrs. Smith rid herself of that reminder by giving you away as a wedding present. You went with your new owners to Macon, thirteen miles away from Maria.

But at least you managed to remain close to your mother—your William was nowhere near as fortunate. His father and mother, then a sister and a brother were all sold off separately. He has not seen them since.

You and William have no children—and you will

not bear any if they cannot be born free. You will not risk seeing them sold away from you, or having them witness either of you on the auction block. You insist on freedom before children.

This mutual desire for a family inspired you and William to concoct your bold plan for escape. It came together in just four days and was steeped from the very beginning in the understanding that your light skin and privileged speech alone were not enough. A white woman traveling with a colored man—slave or not—would have drawn unwanted attention.

Hence the disguise, which William was able to acquire thanks to his own status. As a carpenter hired out around Macon by his owner—and with a second job as a waiter—he had both the opportunity and the spending money to buy this hat, this cloak, these spectacles, and whatnot. He picked them up here and there, so as not to make any single merchant suspicious. The trousers, you made yourself.

The money William saved has paid for your transportation as well. But you could never have boarded that first train in Macon if the two of you hadn't gained your owners' trust. More to the point, you gained their permission to spend a few days away before Christmas to visit your ailing aunt twelve miles off.

During the sleepless night before you left, William cut your long hair. You donned the sling for your arm and the one covering your smooth, hairless chin, with a poultice in each for added effect. The handkerchief beneath your jaw gives you good reason not to talk much, and on top of that, you've been perfectly willing to discourage conversation by pretending to be deaf.

Your invalid's getup makes it easier for other travelers to see what they are inclined to see instead of what you actually are. To them it is more plausible that this gentleman in his early twenties would be afflicted with the rheumatism (and deafness, and heaven knows what else) than that a woman would be so improper as to dress as a man or that a slave would be so clever as to attempt such a deception.

Still, each time you prepare to step onto the platform or wharf, you must steel yourself. Who knows what unwanted attention the sight of you and William together might attract? Who knows who might be waiting?

The train is approaching Richmond now—time to sit up and hope for the best. Before he exits your compartment, the older gentleman hands you a card with some writing on it. He tells you it's a can't-miss recipe for a rheumatism cure.

You thank him, and you take it, and without a glance—without spending even a moment risking that you're "reading" it upside down—you put it in your vest pocket. There is no such thing as being too careful.

SUNDAY, DECEMBER 24, 1848
BALTIMORE, MARYLAND

Earlier this evening, your train from Washington pulled into the hodgepodge of buildings that make up Baltimore's station. This will be your fifth straight night of little or no sleep.

There's the danger that in your fatigue you'll slip up. That you'll say the wrong thing, give yourself away. You long for sleep, but there's a danger there as well. What potential threat might you miss while you doze? And so you force yourself to stay awake.

Baltimore is the last major slave city between you and freedom. It's the last best chance slave catchers have to nab runaways before they get to Pennsylvania.

If you and William get caught, how many ticks of the clock will you have together before you are pulled apart for all time? Whatever is left of your lives after that will surely be made unbearable. But unbearable compared to what? To life as a slave, as a belonging of someone else? Unbearable compared to this self-imposed childlessness? Compared to knowing that you had a plan to liberate yourselves but could not muster the courage to carry it out?

This whole business has had scared you to death from the beginning, but the thought of staying behind scared you something worse.

You've had other fears as well—perhaps not so different from those of other travelers, but magnified by your situation. Pickpockets, for instance. The work of a light-fingered thief in busy places such as this could leave you and William destitute and at even greater risk. So you have kept your own pockets empty while William carries your money. Who would think to pick a slave's pockets?

William has just helped you to your train car, gotten you situated, and left for his own car when he returns, quite unexpectedly. There is a railroad officer, he says, who wants to speak with Mr. Johnson.

Doesn't the railroad officer know that poor Mr. Johnson just wants to get to Philadelphia? Still, you go with William to the bustling office. The situation, whatever it is, does not sound good. It sounds like another opportunity for your plot to be discovered and for you and William to be removed from each other. You are so tired—can you summon the cleverness and clarity that the moment requires?

"Do you wish to see me, sir?" you ask.

Indeed he does. "It is against our rules, sir, to allow any person to take a slave out of Baltimore into Philadelphia, unless he can satisfy us that he has a right to take him along."

Well?

Ellen?

You speak to him with a forcefulness never before possible for you in a conversation with a white man.

"Why is that?" you demand.

He explains: What if this slave does not really belong to you? What if the slave's rightful owner later comes along? The railroad would have to pay the slave owner for his lost property.

The increasingly attentive crowd is on your side— that is, on the side of this young Southern gentleman who obviously has enough problems as it is without the Baltimore & Ohio railroad piling on another.

Don't you know anyone in Baltimore who can vouch for you? asks the B&O man.

Excitement and fear throb in your veins.

"No," you tell him. "I bought tickets in Charleston to pass us through to Philadelphia, and therefore you have no right to detain us here."

"Well, sir," the officer insists, "right or no right, we shan't let you go."

A bell rings. It is time for your train to pull out. And under this new pressure, your adversary begins to waver.

"I really don't know what to do," he confesses. He is not prepared to detain you. But what will happen to him if he's wrong?

He caves.

"Let this gentleman and slave pass," he tells a clerk. "As he is not well, it is a pity to stop him here. We will let him go."

Moments later, you are back in your car, and William is making his way back to his own. God willing, before the sun comes up, you will be on free soil.

LATER THAT NIGHT
HAVRE DE GRACE, MARYLAND

In your weariness, the sudden shuffling about of people and their belongings is disorienting. It's around midnight, maybe seventy miles shy of Philadelphia, and they're getting you and the rest of the first-class passengers off the train.

Where is William? Why isn't he here to help you this time?

They're guiding you all toward a ferry to cross the Susquehanna River.

Where is William?

On the other side, they say, awaits the train that will take you to Philadelphia. But where is William?

It's cold. It's raining. Is it still Christmas Eve, or is it now Christmas Day?

Where is William?

You ask the conductor about your slave. But your

disguise has worked too well. This Northerner clearly sides with the abolitionists—he has no sympathy for your human-owning kind.

"I haven't seen anything of him in some time," he tells you. "I have no doubt he has run away and is in Philadelphia, free, long before now."

You know this cannot be. You plead with the conductor to help you.

"I am no slave hunter," the conductor replies.

You're on your own.

If you get off this train, there's no getting back on. You have no money.

Is he captured? Has he been killed? Where is William?

Where is your William?

Where is he?

WHAT HAPPENED NEXT?

ELLEN CRAFT'S TERROR in Havre de Grace was real but short-lived. She was reunited with her husband on the other side of the Susquehanna that night—he had fallen asleep in the luggage car. They celebrated their first day of freedom in Philadelphia on Christmas Day. The circumstances of their escape made the Crafts celebrities among abolitionists in the Northeast but, threatened by slave hunters, they soon moved to England. There, they had five children, got formal educations, gave lectures about their experiences, and wrote their story as *Running a Thousand Miles for Freedom*. Proceeds from the book allowed William Craft to buy his mother and a sister out of slavery; later, Ellen's mother moved across the Atlantic to join the Crafts. After the Civil War, Ellen and William returned to Georgia and opened a school for former slaves, whom they taught to read, write, and pursue trades such as carpentry and sewing. Ellen died in 1897, William in 1900.

BLACK MAN? WHITE MAN?
JOHN HOWARD GRIFFIN

1935, TOURS, FRANCE

You are a fifteen-year-old Texas boy in France for the first time. You have arrived weeks before the dorm opens at your boarding school, and you don't have enough money to rent a room. You do not speak French.

1943, SOLOMON ISLANDS

Your mission on this remote island is simple. Your job is to secure the natives' cooperation with the Allies in case fighting with the Japanese flares up again. You're learning the islanders' language, and you're learning their customs, but you rely on a five-year-old to guide you through the jungle.

1947
MANSFIELD, TEXAS

You are unpacking your bags here at your parents' new home, feeling around for where things go. It took years for that exploding shell in the South Pacific to finish doing its damage to you, but now it's done. You have finally lost the last of your eyesight. You cannot see a thing.

LATE NOVEMBER 1959
MONTGOMERY, ALABAMA

You once were blind, but now you see. You were black, but now you're white.

Your blindness miraculously ended after a decade of darkness. Your blackness began just this month, and it was no miracle. It was deliberate.

You set out on an assignment for *Sepia* magazine—a white man crisscrossing Louisiana, Mississippi, and Alabama with artificially darkened skin. It's not that there's a shortage of writers with God-given pigment and God-given talent. No, there are plenty of Negro writers capable of detailing the torments and indignities of daily life in a land where civil rights are still a revolutionary concept.

Thanks to your disguise, what you can see—and nobody else can—is the *contrast* between life lived black and life lived white. And though you've known more than your share of unfamiliar, unsettling situations, none has been more bewildering than this one.

You have felt at least as alien in your own land as you did in France and the Pacific. Nothing you've seen these past few weeks, however, can compare to what your eyes are witnessing here in Montgomery.

You arrived in town by bus just before Thanksgiving. The inhumane treatment you've endured from whites has taken its toll, and—perversely, perhaps— you've decided to rejoin them.

Even before you got here, you quit taking the Oxsoralen pills. Now you keep indoors during the daytime, staying out of the sun so that its rays can't interact with the residual medication that would maintain your shade of brown. As the Oxsoralen and its resulting pigment work their way out of your system, you scrub at the stain you applied to your skin's outer layers, shedding the darkened cells at the surface to make way for the pinker ones below.

You put on a white shirt, but it makes your skin

look too dark by comparison. So you put on a brown one—there, that's better—and venture into the white part of town.

There you find that all the comforts of a white man's everyday life—a policeman's friendly greeting, an open table in a restaurant—are once again available to you, though impossible to take for granted or enjoy.

Now you stroll into a black neighborhood, and what do you find? The people you pass on the street are looking at you—the white John Howard Griffin—with the same hate-stare that the black John Howard Griffin had come to expect from whites. You no longer sense from Negroes a shared, unspoken understanding—that automatic intimacy is gone, reflexive resentment in its place.

You aren't dressed any differently than you've been previously on this journey, aren't using a different name, aren't claiming any different biographical details other than the obvious one. This is all about the color of your skin. And you just know that, why, if you were to suddenly be black again right now . . .

Now *there's* an idea. The novelty, the recklessness of it are invigorating.

You think of it as "zigzagging." You've returned with a bag in which you've stashed skin dye, a sponge, cold cream, and tissues. A comic-book superhero and his alter ego may transform in a phone booth, but the white you and the black you need a little more seclusion for your quick changes.

Into an alley, white to black, and then you're meandering about as a second-class citizen, befriended by Negroes and disregarded by whites.

Then, behind some bushes by the side of a road, black to white, and you begin retracing your steps as a person of privilege, embraced by other whites and instantly distanced from Montgomery's black citizens.

The white people you walk among have no idea that you have lived as a black man. It would never occur to them that any white person would make such a choice. Darkening up to get easy laughs from a crowd, now, that's one thing. But to assume the *identity* of one of them . . .

And when you pass those same white people while playing the role of Negro, well, let's just say it doesn't call for much in the way of acting skills. Their hostility toward you—or, at the very best, neglect—has nothing to do with how you act or who you are, and everything to do with how you look.

The same goes for the treatment you get while white among blacks. Would a closer inspection of you reveal a darker skin tone than that of other white passersby? A lingering hint of stain that could be misread as evidence of a Negro grandmother or great-grandfather? Perhaps. But you've learned enough of the distance black folks keep for their own self-preservation whenever they can, enough to know that none of them will get that close. You *look* white, and so you *are* white. It is as simple as that.

But what if? What if someone recognizes your shoes as those worn yesterday by a black man who was—say!—just about your height? Or what if someone catches you in mid-transformation? What would they make of you? Would they quake with anger and dismay? Would getting caught in the act of crossing over or crossing back be even more dangerous than being black all the time?

In the Pacific, you knew what it was like to have your life in jeopardy, and you're not eager to experience that again. But you had a mission then, and you have a mission now. You suffered the consequences then, and you'll risk now what you have to risk. During the ten years you lived in darkness, you came to understand that skin color could not possibly be less relevant. Perhaps if you carry on your masquerade just a little bit longer, the story you'll tell will be just a little bit more powerful and enable that many more people to see the truth.

You know what you have to do.

You'll be black again soon enough, at least for another day, but you'll never again be blind.

WHAT HAPPENED NEXT?

JOHN HOWARD GRIFFIN ended his experimental journey through the South on December 14, 1959. He returned home to Texas, where he began writing his account of that journey, eventually published as the book *Black Like Me*. Griffin was modest about his accomplishment: "This may not be all of it," his book began. *Black Like Me* became a classic—and occasionally banned—work in American literature; it also prompted death threats. Griffin died of various ailments in 1980.

RISING TEENAGE STAR?
RILEY WESTON

WEDNESDAY, OCTOBER 14, 1998
LOS ANGELES, CALIFORNIA

You just wanted to work.

You would have wanted to work, to be an actor, no matter what you looked like. The fact that you still look like a teenager, or close enough, shouldn't be important. But it's not just *important*.

It's *everything*.

Biologically, you became a teenager in 1979, on the day that Kimberlee Elizabeth Seaman turned thirteen. Nearly two decades later, you go by the name of Riley Weston, but you're still playing the part of an adolescent—not only on this L.A. set, but in your real life.

Your audience is the biggest it's ever been. By this time tomorrow, it's going to be even bigger. Much bigger. And there's nothing you can do to stop it.

* * *

Here's how it started:

You grew up in little-bitty, two-stoplight, Pleasant Valley, New York. From the time you were, like, four years old, you wanted to be an entertainer, visible, *on stage*. In high school, you did drama, chorus, student government, and cheerleading, a dynamo just shy of five feet tall.

And what do girls with dreams like yours do when they graduate high school? They go to L.A. They change their names to something like "Kimberlee Kramer." They babysit to pay the bills, and they audition, audition, and audition some more.

All that work started to pay off for you. You did commercials. You got the lead in a musical for troubled teens and their therapists. You were "Nice Car Girl" in a movie about competitive waterskiing, and "Rita Sabatini" in a couple of episodes of ABC's *Growing Pains*. In 1993 you were in *Sister Act 2*, starring Whoopi Goldberg, which was *huge* for you.

The thing is, they had you playing a kid. They *all* had you playing kids. Here you were entering your late twenties, and the roles you kept getting were, like, "Girl Number Whatever." But you still looked the part, and if it was those parts or none at all, what were you going to do? Of *course* you took the work.

And if you shaved a few years off your age so you

could get a foot in the door at the auditions, well, who *didn't?* That's the way show business works—new names, fudged ages, closeted actors, fake boobs. That's just Hollywood, and you were determined.

Along the way, Brad Sexton became your manager. You also married the guy. He wasn't a big name, but then, neither were you—maybe you'd get to the top together. And by last year, you each had some ideas about how to make that happen.

It was one thing to still be getting teenage roles in your thirties. It was another to be getting *crappy* teenage roles, these insulting, one-dimensional parts. You were a serious actor, and you needed better scripts, and if nobody out there was going to offer them to you, you would just have to write them yourself. You'd never done that before, but you knew you could figure out how. So you added another hyphen and became an actor-singer-writer.

Nobody cares, really, how old a screenwriter is. Being thirty-one as a writer would be no big deal. But you couldn't be a thirty-one-year-old writer *and* be an actor young enough to land the teenage parts you'd be writing for yourself. You needed one identity for both of those facets of your career.

Since someone might notice that "Kimberlee Kramer" had been playing teenagers for a decade already, Brad persuaded you that this single identity should be a new one. Actors change their names all the time—again, no big deal. Except for one thing: Your new legal name, Riley Weston, would come with a fake I.D. showing that you were a teenager. Having a phony I.D. was not so normal. That was a little unusual, actually.

But you tried it, and you wrote and wrote and wrote some more. For a long time, you didn't do much else, and you came up with a really good spec script for the pilot episode of a TV drama. You called it *Holliman's Way*, and it's about these three teenage sisters, and Brad sent it to this producer who really liked it and wanted to meet with you. He didn't even know how old you were supposed to be—he just liked your writing.

At this meeting, the producer didn't want to talk just about *Holliman's Way*—he wanted to talk about *you*, and your background, and how this tiny eighteen-year-old actress with no credits to her name came to be sitting in a Hollywood producer's office discussing her script. Kimberlee Kramer's story wouldn't do, of course—Riley Weston needed one of her own. So you told him you'd been homeschooled, and that your mom had brought you out here, that you'd arrived a couple of years ago, when you were sixteen.

Things started happening fast. That producer sent your script to a director, and he liked it too—he didn't know your age either—but that turned out to be a dead end. Brad kept shopping *Holliman's Way* around, though, and this huge talent agency signed you up. And this past spring, they got you a six-month, $60,000 contract as a writer for a new TV series that would debut in the fall.

Felicity.

You were *perfect* for it—the main character is this girl Felicity who's just going off to college, so having an eighteen-year-old writer on the staff made total sense. The other writers were all older than that. Even the star was already in her twenties. The two guys who created the show were about the same age as you—the same age you *really* are. Everybody working on the scripts had a lot more writing experience than you, but while sometimes you felt like you were just along for the ride, they turned to you for help in getting the characters' late-adolescent voices right.

You had to keep in mind that as far as they knew, you actually *were* an eighteen-year-old—and a fairly naive one at that. You needed to act the part—bringing in stuffed animals for your office, hanging up a *Titanic* poster, talking about boys. Everyone on the show threw a big party for you right there on the set for your nineteenth birthday.

Playing that role all day long month after month was exhausting. They all knew that what you most wanted to do was act, but they had no idea how much acting you were already doing.

The show was really coming together, though, and this past summer, before the first episode even aired, *Felicity* was getting a lot of buzz. Part of that was because the network figured that having an actual teenager on the writing staff of a show about teenagers would make a good story, and they pitched it to the media. But what *Entertainment Weekly* did was a little surprising.

The magazine has this feature they do each June called "The It List," which is a rundown of the hottest, most creative actors and writers and singers in the business. And out of everyone involved in *Felicity*, it was *you* they wrote about. They singled you out. When they interviewed you, you told them, "In many ways, I am Felicity," though you never said exactly what those ways were—or weren't.

A *lot* of people read *Entertainment Weekly*—people outside Hollywood, in airports and supermarkets and doctors' offices, everywhere. Riley Weston suddenly became a lot better known than Kimberlee Kramer ever was, and no one besides insiders had even actually seen *Felicity* yet. By the time the show did go on the air at the end of last month, something even bigger had come your way: a $300,000 deal to create shows about teenagers for Disney/Touchstone. *Holliman's Way* might actually happen after all.

Meanwhile, your big break as an actress came along. An episode of *Felicity* you helped write has this character—a visiting high school junior named Story Zimmer who's totally single-minded about getting what she wants, which in her case is to go clubbing—and she's you, really. She's you. It's a subplot, but she's got four big scenes, and they're all comic relief breaking up this really heavy storyline about date rape, and people always remember the funny parts. You auditioned for the role, and you *nailed* it.

So, things are going great, right? *Entertainment Weekly*. Touchstone. *The Wall Street Journal* is interviewing you, and *Entertainment Tonight* is following you around the set. You've got a big role—you shot the first half of the Story episode just yesterday.

And then . . .

And then . . .

And then somebody turns on you. Somebody turns you in. Someone starts calling the show's producers and your talent agency and reporters and everyone and telling who you really are, how old you really are, how long you've been around. They even have your Social Security number, and they've been giving that out so that reporters can see the proof down at the courthouse where you changed your name.

You don't know who is making those calls. Or why. Why would they *do* that?

You're here in your dressing room on the set of *Felicity*, on what ought to be the greatest day of your whole life. You've worked for thirteen, fourteen years to have scenes like these to shoot—scenes that you're at the center of, scenes where millions of people are going to pay attention to you. You ought to be getting ready for the shoot.

But instead, you've got this message from a reporter. She's the one who wrote the "Touchstone TV inks teen scribe" article last week, but today she seems so hostile. You know that the producers know—you knew before you even showed up today that you were going to have to face them.

But you can't deal with that right now. You just can't worry about it. You're a professional actor, and you've got to keep it together at least long enough to complete your scenes. And then—well, who knows what then?

You know, though—this whole thing would really make an excellent TV movie. If only they would let you play yourself.

WHAT HAPPENED NEXT?

RILEY WESTON INSPIRED a brief stretch of soul-searching in Hollywood about the bias toward younger talent and why some sorts of showbiz deceptions are more acceptable than others. Weston's own career suffered, and her later acting and writing efforts attracted much less attention than her work on *Felicity*. In 2006, as she entered her forties, she published a novel, *Before I Go*, about a teenage ice skater with terminal cancer. She hoped it would become a movie, starring herself.

26-YEAR-OLD WITH SUFFICIENT FUNDS? FRANK W. ABAGNALE JR.

SPRING 1964

NEW YORK CITY

Boy, *that* was easy.

You're no master con artist. You're no master anything, actually. You're just a sixteen-year-old runaway
with a lot of gall. But it looks like that just might be
enough to get by on.

That money in your hand couldn't have been easier
to come by—you wrote a check out to "CASH," the
teller handed over the bills, and the bank is just micro-
scopically worse off than it would have been if you'd
never walked in the door. So what if, technically, there's
not actually any money left in the account behind that

check? And so what if, truth be told, you're not really the twenty-six-year-old the teller thought you were?

You needed something the bank had, the bank needed it less than you did, and nobody got hurt. Easy.

Easy, that is, once you overlook the hard situation that got you where you are in the first place. No, not just hard—devastating. Your parents had separated for a while, and then one day, without warning, they called you out of school and down to family court. Before you'd fully grasped what was going on—and without so much as looking at you—the judge asked you which parent you wanted to live with after the divorce.

What kind of question is that? Well, in your case, it's the kind of question that you answered by running away, leaving Westchester County that very day and heading twenty-five miles south to Manhattan. You didn't take much with you, but you did bring the essentials:

Your driver's license.

A book of personalized checks for that $200 bank account your dad opened for you a while back.

Your own six-foot-tall, prematurely gray-haired self.

That's right—gray-haired already, just like your dad. It started when you were fifteen, and it's the number one reason folks always think you're older than you really are. Not having any acne helps too.

Anyway, you knew midtown Manhattan well from

making deliveries for your dad's stationery store at Fortieth and Madison. And when you got to midtown, all you wanted was to get by. You were even prepared to do it honestly, though that scam you pulled back home with your dad's Mobil gas card—charging set after set of tires, then selling them back to the dealers for 2,500 bucks in cash—showed a certain flair for other approaches.

You rented a boarding room by the day and started looking for a job. But what you found was a fairly limited set of career opportunities for a sixteen-year-old dropout—imagine that. So the obvious solution was to not be a sixteen-year-old dropout. Maybe you could have forged a high school diploma and passed yourself off as a precocious adolescent with a go-get-'em attitude. But you chose a simpler route. Why fake a whole document when you can fudge just one teensy little number?

Without much effort, and definitely without anything resembling a *plan*, you turned back the clock on your date of birth: On your pictureless driver's license, you changed the 1948 to 1938. Now you were twenty-six-year-old Frank W. Abagnale Jr. Trouble is, the twenty-six-year-old version of Frank Abagnale was just as much of a high school dropout as the sixteen-year-old version. More employable, perhaps, but as you soon found out, getting employed and getting decent pay are two very different things. Your income wasn't nearly enough to keep you afloat in Manhattan.

All along, of course, you were tapping into that $200 account. A $15 check cashed here, a $25 check cashed there—you kept them as small as you could, but those numbers added up. Within a week or two of your arrival in the city, your account has been drawn down to nothing.

Which is where you are today—or rather, where you *were* until just now, as you casually make for the bank exit.

Who would have thought that you could just write a check no matter how little money—if any—was behind it? If this giant bank doesn't want to be taken advantage of, it shouldn't make it so easy.

All you had to do was ad-lib a story for the teller, something along the lines of how you lost your bag containing your wallet but luckily had your checkbook in your back pocket: "I don't have an account here, and I need to get home on the train. I don't have any money. Could somebody cash a check for me?"

"No sir, I can't do that," she replied, "but if you go over to see that man behind the desk, he may cash it for you."

The man behind the desk took pity on you. He put his initials on the check and said, "Give this back to the teller and she'll cash it for you."

Piece of cake. You didn't even have to show a photo I.D., for crying out loud—Frank W. Abagnale Jr. (even the sixteen-year-old version) could look like anyone, and nobody would be the wiser.

In the days since, you've repeated that con again and again. And as you emerge from a bank with that ill-gotten cash in your pocket, you know that not everyone can do what you do. Yes, at night you cry yourself to sleep—you were big enough to leave home, but you hadn't been too big to have your dad kiss you good night right up until the end. In the daylight, though, you've got confidence that most people just don't.

Something about you makes those bank tellers take your checks more seriously than they do the average Joe's—makes them take your checks, period. You've always been at ease around grown-ups. In fact, you've preferred their company to that of kids your age, and your comfort with adults must show. They don't even look at your checks, really—they look at you, your height, your hair, and give you exactly what you want.

Are you reckless? Sure. After all, those checks have your real name and hometown address. You don't even question the wisdom of sticking around midtown, where you might be seen by one of the customers you used to make deliveries to for your dad—or even get seen by your dad himself. It's the part of Manhattan you're most familiar with, so at least for now, that's where you stay.

Common sense says that even in a town as big as

New York, you're going to run out of places to bounce your rubber checks sooner or later. But the thing is, you're still just sixteen. Not actually old enough to vote or join the army—or to drink, even if you wanted to—you aren't entirely sure you're ready to head out to another city. And even if you are up to it, you aren't eager to find yourself in a town where bank tellers aren't as friendly to a New York State driver's license.

You think about this for a while. You think about nothing *but* this for a while. And it's surely on your mind, even if it's at the back, as you walk up Forty-second Street—just a couple of blocks from your dad's store—one afternoon amid the five o'clock hustle and traffic.

Right now, back home in Westchester County, guys your age are shooting hoops and spinning Beatles 45s. You, you're fifty-five minutes and another world away. You're strolling past the Commodore Hotel when a car pulls up in front. Out steps an Eastern Airlines pilot and his crew.

Heads turn. Doors open. Respect is shown.

Is anyone else at this scene thinking what you're thinking? That nobody's *ever* going to seriously question that man in uniform before cashing his check?

And is anyone else here wondering what you're wondering? Which is: Just how old do you have to be to pass for an airline pilot?

About twenty-six, is your guess.

WHAT HAPPENED NEXT?

FRANK ABAGNALE JR. had barely begun. Between the ages of sixteen and twenty-one and under a bevy of names, he posed as a pilot (never actually piloting a plane), a doctor (never actually practicing medicine), lawyer, Secret Service agent, and so forth, passing bad checks and conning banks out of millions of dollars. Frank wasn't delusional—he knew he would get caught, and he did. After a brutal stint in a French prison, he began a decades-long career training FBI agents to detect fraud and teaching banks how to improve security.

AFTERWORD
CHRIS BARTON

NOVEMBER 2010
AUSTIN, TEXAS

Who do you think you are?

Really, you ask yourself, just who do you think you are? You've got some nerve thinking you can get inside the heads of the ten people you've written about in this book. And where do you get off thinking you can put the readers inside those people's heads as well?

But wait—it's not like you picked these ten people at random. There were other candidates, other impostors and pretenders that you considered, but their stories and circumstances didn't offer what you needed in order to tell their stories this way.

And what you needed was documentation—details of these masquerades captured in a personal way, or a public way, or both. These people's memoirs, interviews, and public statements were useful, to the extent that you could trust them; after all, we're talking about people who made their mark by misleading folks. Police reports, news accounts, and the tellings of others were helpful too, though these sources were often based either on statements grabbed amid the hubbub and swirl at the end of the deception, or on memories tapped months, years, or even decades after the incident.

So, let's face it, all of these profiles are imperfect. There are undoubtedly things you got wrong, or didn't get right enough. But through the telling of all ten of these stories, and through your attempts to understand all ten of these lives, you feel like you've gained something that a lifetime spent delving into every last detail of only one of these stories would not offer.

Now, you ought to state right up front that you're not inclined to go out and take on a fake identity or pretend to be someone else. But if you were, you think you have a pretty good idea now of how to go about it successfully. ("Successfully" is a relative term, of course. More than half of your subjects were caught in the act—if they hadn't been, we might never have known about them.)

Some key lessons:

1. *Look the part.* Getting fooled by one of these masqueraders was often just a matter of looking only at the surface—seeing a Transit Authority uniform shirt and a bag of motorman's gear was to see a T.A. employee,

not a teenager with a thing for trains; seeing a light-skinned person in a gentleman's clothes was to see a white man, not an African American woman. It's like Frank Abagnale told you: "All they saw standing in front of them was this uniform—not the person *in* the uniform, but the uniform."

2. *Let your would-be discoverers feel smart*. People who feel smarter when they're around you tend to have fond feelings for you and will be less inclined to question whether you really are who you say you are. Ferdinand Waldo Demara Jr., as "Dr. Joseph Cyr" and in his other guises, had a real knack for making experts in his fields of fakery feel this way. How did he do it? Get this: He asked their opinions and listened to what they had to say. He got information he needed, and they got an ego boost.

The mere presence of "Princess Caraboo" (aka Mary Baker) had a similar effect on people—especially on men, apparently. In her silence and in the mystery of her origins, her visitors saw an opportunity to spout whatever random facts or bits of hearsay they had accumulated about the Far East while passing it off as actual knowledge. The more intelligent they made themselves feel, the more material she had to pick and choose from in wordlessly crafting her backstory.

3. *Keep your mouth shut*. The less you say, and especially the less made-up stuff you say, the less you

have to keep track of, and the less likely it is that a listener will begin tugging at an inconsistency in your story in order to see what unravels. Solomon Perel got lucky that it was his Nazi girlfriend's mother, and not his girlfriend herself, with whom he was more talkative than careful.

But in addition to knowing a lot about how to get away with a false identity, you've also learned quite a bit about what to expect from the experience. And it's not something you're eager to try for yourself.

You think of the loneliness. Ellen Craft and Riley Weston were exceptions—they had partners in their deception. The rest were on their own, whether alone in a huge but impersonal crowd (like Frank Abagnale, crying himself to sleep in Manhattan) or in the uncomfortably close company of others (you're not the first to wonder how Sarah Rosetta Wakeman handled getting her period in the barracks). Putting on an act means putting up a wall around you, revealing next to nothing about your true self, and not having a completely honest conversation with anyone. Maybe that's some people's idea of a good time, but it's not yours.

You think of the stress. Solomon Perel must have had it the worst of them all. For *years* he had to maintain that false identity or die. What he said, what he didn't say, how he looked, how he acted, regardless of whether he was awake or asleep—all were potential giveaways, and the toll that must have taken on his nerves is hard to fathom. Mary Baker must have experienced some of the same, and while it would have been nowhere near as severe, who can blame her for running off? Ace Carter and Ferdinand Demara may have been heavy drinkers no matter what their circumstances were, but living lives of deception could not have helped.

You think of the fear. In the case of Craft and Perel and John Howard Griffin, the fear was mortal: Getting caught might well mean getting killed. Even when the stakes of the masquerade were lower—Riley Weston's quest for better TV and movie roles comes to mind—there was the risk of losing out on a life that had been desperately dreamed of and tirelessly worked for. And while it's easy to laugh now at Keron Thomas's predicament while the A train was stuck on the tracks—with the ride of a lifetime literally brought to a screeching halt because he exceeded a twenty-mph speed limit, and his technical skill undone by the lack of a flashlight—you think your own response to that situation would have been to panic. Just a little, of course.

You also think of what life held in store for these ten when their masquerades ended—though you've tried not to. None of them knew, in the moments you've worked to capture, what would happen to them in the minutes that followed or in years to come, and so you've deliberately tried to block out your own knowledge of their futures.

It seems only fair to recognize, however, that their lives amounted to more than their deceptions. But it's useful too. Because now that you think about it, you see that where these people ended up—all over the map— echoes the motivations behind their masquerades.

Better pay, better jobs, easy money, social justice, psychological need, plain old-fashioned kicks, sheer survival—each of those motives, plus others that you've no doubt missed, can be found in at least one of these stories. Take another ten masqueraders and you'd probably find as many more.

Which brings up one more question. These subjects all had *their* reasons for pretending to be someone else. Can you imagine what *yours* would be?

ACKNOWLEDGMENTS

Writing the paragraphs below has reminded me of what a generous world this can be, and I'm glad to have the opportunity to say so.

Special thanks goes to those who made time for interviews for this project—not only Frank Abagnale and Keron Thomas, but also author and filmmaker Laura Browder, journalist Jenny Hontz, chess coach (and former T.A. motorman) Regoberto Sabio, and Ferdinand Waldo Demara's high school acquaintance Irene Wolfendon and his *Cayuga* shipmates Peter Chance, Bill Doyle, Ted Meyers, and Don Saxon.

Many others provided additional support for my research, and I am grateful to each one of them, including Benton Arnovitz and Aleisa Fishman at the United States Holocaust Memorial Museum, Robert Bonazzi, Steve Campbell at *County Magazine*, Deirdre Castle at the Victoria *Times Colonist*, Sarah Davis at the Baltimore & Ohio Railroad Museum, Nekeela DeHaarte,

James Fleming, Carrie Ann Flora, Marie Ford at Central Catholic High School, Beatrice Hotchin, Rebecca Smith Hurd, John LaFave at Cengage Learning, Joan LeFosse at ABC News, Ryan Mackey at the Cherokee Nation Cultural Resource Center, George Moore at the Naval Officers Association of Canada, Maren Nelson at Brown University Alumni Relations, Douglas Newman, the community at NYC Transit Forums, Marco Ricci, Marc Tyler Nobleman, Jeff Robel at the National Climatic Data Center, Bernard Spaughton, Kelly Welbes at Abagnale & Associates, John White at the College of Charleston Library, and Jennifer Ziegler.

Thanks also to the indispensible staffs at the libraries of Austin, Texas; Columbia University; Kingston, Ontario; Lawrence, Massachusetts; New York City; the University of Texas; and Washington, D.C., and to those at Library and Archives Canada and the State of Alabama Department of Archives and History, and to all those who spent time on my various Freedom of Information Act and Interlibrary Loan requests.

Wow. That's a lot of people who helped just with my gathering of the raw materials for this book. My wife and sons may have realized before I did that this project was like researching and writing ten different picture book biographies (and then some) at the same time. Thank you, and you, and you for being so understanding and accommodating and supportive.

Editors Judy O'Malley and Nancy Mercado and my

agent, Erin Murphy, showed the initial enthusiasm for this project that propelled it into the hands of Alisha Niehaus, its even-more-enthusiastic editor and all-around champion at Dial Books. Heather Alexander at Dial deserves the credit for coming up with the book's title, after it had gone through almost as many temporary names as Demara. Thank you all, and the rest of the crew at Dial for their parts in bringing this book about, and Jean Dayton at Dayton Bookings for her much-needed support during the home stretch.

That Paul Hoppe deserves my thanks and appreciation is self-evident. But Paul also bought me a cup of coffee at New York City's Books of Wonder, and that carries a lot of weight with me too.

Finally, my experience as the writer of these stories was infinitely less lonely than the experiences of my subjects, and much of the credit for that goes to my friends in the children's literature community who read parts of this book and encouraged me onward. Many of those friends and I spent two and a half critique-filled days in the Austin home of Cynthia and Greg Leitich Smith, discussing and debating—among many other things about many other manuscripts—whether the second-person point of view was a good idea to start with and, regardless, how to make it better. I hope I gave as good as I got. Thank you all for your help, and thank you for letting me be myself.

BIBLIOGRAPHY
or,
HOW YOU—ER, *I*—DID IT

KERON THOMAS

Cudahy, Brian J. *Under the Sidewalks of New York: The Story of the Greatest Subway System in the World*. Fordham University Press, Bronx, New York, 1995.

"Day tripper; Teen posing as motorman takes train for joyride in New York City," *Houston Chronicle*, May 11, 1993.

Dougherty, Peter. *Tracks of the New York City Subway*, Third Edition. Self-published, 2003.

Fischler, Stan. *The Subway: A Trip Through Time on New York's Rapid Transit*. H&M Productions II Inc., New York, 1997.

Frankel, Bruce. "NYC teen takes city for a ride; A 3-hour spin on the subway," *USA Today*, May 12, 1993.

Frattini, Dave. *The Underground Guide to New York Subways*. St. Martin's Press, New York, 2000.

Gladwell, Malcolm. "Motorman Takes City For a Ride; B Movie Episode Rolls on A Train," *The Washington Post*, May 12, 1993.

Gregory, Sophfronia Scott and Massimo Calabres. "The great A train robbery," *Time*, May 24, 1993.

Henican, Ellis. "Subway Joyrider Arrested in N.Y.; Teenage rail buff drove train safely through 85 stations," *The San Francisco Chronicle (Newsday)*, May 12, 1993.

———. "Subway joyrider draws probation; New York teen still thrilled by power of trains," *The Evening News Harrisburg (Newsday)*, July 15, 1993.

"Impostor takes A train passengers in N.Y. City for a ride," *Buffalo News* (Associated Press), May 11, 1993.

Kaufman, Michael T. "Don't Take That A Train! Ever! I Mean It, Son!" *The New York Times*, May 15, 1993.

Kennedy, Randy. *Subwayland: Adventures in the World Beneath New York*. St. Martin's Griffin, New York, 2004.

McLarin, Kimberly J. "Subway Caper Fueled by Passion for Trains," *The New York Times*, May 12, 1993.

Pérez-Peña, Richard. "Aficionado Of Subway Spared Prison," *The New York Times*, July 15, 1993.

Sabio, Regoberto. Telephone interviews with author, December 9, 2009, and December 13, 2009.

Sansone, Gene. *New York Subways: An Illustrated History of New York City's Transit Cars*. The Johns Hopkins University Press, Baltimore, 1997.

Swerdlow, Marian. *Underground Woman: My Four Years As a New York City Subway Conductor*. Temple University Press, Philadelphia, 1998.

"Teen takes train on trek he dreamed about," *St. Petersburg Times* (Associated Press), May 12, 1993.

Thomas, Keron. Telephone interviews with author, October 26, 2009, and December 18, 2009.

Thomas, Robert McG. Jr. "Lawbreakers We Have Known and Loved," *The New York Times*, May 16, 1993.

Weir, Richard. "Fame, Fleeting Fame, Found These New Yorkers. Then What Happened?" *The New York Times*, December 27, 1998.

"Youth gets probation for train joy ride," *Buffalo News* (Associated Press), July 15, 1993.

FERDINAND WALDO DEMARA JR.

"All at Sea," *Time*, December 3, 1951.

Allen, Mel. "Notable New England Fraud; The man who broke North Haven's heart," *Yankee Magazine*, September 1989.

Burton, Sarah. *Impostors: Six Kinds of Liar*. Viking, London, 2000.

Chance, Peter. "Dentistry by Proxy," *Starshell*, Summer 2007.

———. Telephone interview with author, November 18, 2008.

Coleman, James C. *Abnormal Psychology and Modern Life*. Scott, Foresman, Glenview, Illinois, 1976.

Crichton, Robert. *The Great Impostor/The Rascal and the Road*. Avon Books, New York, 1968.

Doyle, Bill. Telephone interview with author, November 19, 2008.

Federal Bureau of Investigation records provided via Freedom of Information Act on March 26, 2009.

"Ferdinand the Bull Thrower," *Time*, February 25, 1957.

"Ferdinand Waldo Demara, 60, an impostor in varied fields," *The New York Times* (Associated Press), June 9, 1982.

"Ferdinand Waldo Demara; Impostor acted as RCN surgeon," *The Globe and Mail* (Associated Press), June 9, 1982.

"Ferdinand 'Waldo' Demara: The Great Impostor," CFB Esquimalt Naval & Military Museum, accessed at http://www .navalandmilitarymuseum.org/resource_pages/chars/demara .html on November 17, 2009.

Heinz, W. C. "The man with a life in his hands," *Life*, January 20, 1961.

Hotchin, Beatrice. Telephone interview with author, December 15, 2008.

Hurt, Raymond. *The History of Cardiothoracic Surgery from Early Times*. Parthenon Publishing, New York, 1996.

Gaffen, Fred. *Cross-Border Warriors: Canadians in American Forces, Americans in Canadian Forces*. Dundurn Press, Toronto, 1995.

Gardam, John. *Korea Volunteer: An Oral History from Those Who Were There*. General Store Publishing House, Burnstown, Ontario, 1994.

"'He's a Tremendous Man'; Great Imposter Now in Pulpit On San Juan Isle," *Daily Colonist*, January 8, 1970.

Horton, David M. and George R. Nielsen. *Walking George: The Life of George John Beto and the Rise of the Modern Texas Prison System*. University of North Texas Press, Denton, Texas, 2005.

"Impostor here for reunion," *Daily Colonist*, September 2, 1979.

MacAdam, Pat. "The Great Impostor's last victim: Fred Demara lived his life in a blur of impersonations—a doctor, a teacher, a Catholic brother and more," *The Ottawa Citizen*, April 11, 1999.

McCarthy, Joe. "The master impostor: an incredible tale; Expert at hoaxes tops colorful career by becoming famous Canadian naval surgeon," *Life*, January 26, 1952.

"'A man bitten by an imp'; Great Impostor dies at 60," *Times-Colonist*, June 9, 1982.

Medical Department, United States Army. *Surgery in World War II: Thoracic Surgery*, Volumes 1 and 2. Office of the Surgeon General, Department of the Army, Washington, D.C., 1963.

Meissner, Dirk. "Man who discovered doctor was Great Imposter dies at

70," *Times-Colonist*, February 6, 1991.

Melady, John. *Korea: Canada's Forgotten War*. Macmillan of Canada, Toronto, 1983.

Meyers, Edward C. Telephone interview with author, December 2, 2008.

———. *Thunder in the Morning Calm*. Vanwell, St. Catharines, Ontario, 1992.

Peate, Les. "The Case of the Spurious Sawbones," Korea Veterans Association of Canada (*Esprit de Corps Magazine*), accessed online at http://www.kvacanada.com/stories_lpimposter.htm on November 17, 2009.

"The Persistent Phony," *Newsweek*, February 25, 1957.

Pollio, Howard R. *Behavior and Existence*. Brooks/Cole, Monterey, California, 1982.

Robertson, Ian. "James Plomer," *County Magazine*, Winter 1979.

———. "'Victim' fondly remembers Great Imposter," *The Whig-Standard*, June 9, 1982.

Saxon, Don. Telephone interview with author, November 19, 2008.

Thorgrimsson, Thor and Edward C. Russell. *Canadian Naval Operations in Korean Waters, 1950–1955*. The Naval Historical Section, Canadian Forces Headquarters, Department of National Defence, Ottawa, 1965.

Tonight Starring Jack Paar, November 16, 1962. *The Jack Paar Collection*. Sony Shout, 2004. DVD.

Weber, Tom. "The Great Impostor; One man's years of brilliant deception came to an end on small Maine island," *Bangor Daily News*, June 7, 1997.

Wolfendon, Irene. Telephone interview with author, April 28, 2010.

PRIVATE WAKEMAN

Blanton, DeAnne and Lauren M. Cook. *They Fought Like Demons: Women Soldiers in the Civil War*. Vintage Books, New York, 2003.

Burgess, Lauren Cook. *An Uncommon Soldier: The Civil War Letters of Sarah Rosetta Wakeman, alias Pvt. Lyons Wakeman, 153rd Regiment, New York State Volunteers, 1862–1864*. Oxford University Press, New York, 1995.

Krick, Robert K. *Civil War Weather in Virginia*. The University of Alabama Press, Tuscaloosa, 2007.

McPherson, James M. *For Cause and Comrades: Why Men Fought in the Civil War*. Oxford University Press, New York, 1997.

Tsui, Bonnie. *She Went to the Field: Women Soldiers of the Civil War*. TwoDot, Guilford, Connecticut, 2003.

Wiley, Bell I. *The Life of Billy Yank: The Common Soldier of the Union*. Book-of-the-Month Club, New York, 1994.

SOLOMON PEREL

Bartoletti, Susan Campbell. *Hitler Youth: Growing Up in Hitler's Shadow*. Scholastic Nonfiction, New York, 2005.

Bartov, Omer. *Hitler's Army: Soldiers, Nazis, and War in the Third Reich*. Oxford University Press, New York, 1991.

Diehl, Jackson. "The Sheep in Wolf's Clothing; Solomon Perel's Double Life as Jew And Nazi, and the Film It Became," *The Washington Post*, March 25, 1992.

Dobroszycki, Lucjan. *The Chronicle of the Lodz Ghetto, 1941–1944*. Yale University Press, New Haven, Connecticut, 1984.

Elkin, Michael. "My life as a Nazi," *Jewish Exponent*, March 5, 1993.

Engelberg, Stephen. "A Life Stranger Than the Movie, 'Europa, Europa,' Based on It," *The New York Times*, February 19, 1992.

Glantz, David M., editor. *The Initial Period of War on the Eastern Front 22 June–August 1941*. Frank Cass, New York, 1993.

Hershenson, Sarah, Kolja Raube, and Andrzej J. Koszyk. "A Life of Two Souls," *The Jerusalem Post Magazine*, August 31, 2001.

Johnson, Eric A. and Karl-Heinz Reuband. *What We Knew: Terror, Mass Murder, and Everyday Life in Nazi Germany*. Basic Books, Cambridge, Massachusetts, 1995.

Kaplan, Marion A. *Between Dignity and Despair: Jewish Life in Nazi Germany*. Oxford University Press, New York, 1998.

"Solomon Perel, At BU, Talks Of Survival," *The Jewish Advocate*, April 1, 1993.

Katz, Leslie. "Real-life hero of Europa Europa to speak in Bay Area," *Jewish Bulletin of Northern California*, October 22, 1993.

Perel, Solomon. *Europa, Europa*. John Wiley & Sons, New York, 1997.

Vancheri, Barbara. "His personal tragedy led to 'Europa, Europa,'" *Pittsburgh Post-Gazette*, March 17, 1993.

"Volkswagen Unveils Plaque to Jewish Hitler Youth Member," *Deutsche Welle*, May 11, 2006.

Yaakov, Yosef. "A Survivor," *Jerusalem Post*, October 1, 1997.

FORREST CARTER

Aicher, Julie. "University Press Gets Bargain From $500 Purchase of Rights to Best Seller," The Associated Press, October 1, 1991.

Barra, Allen. "The education of Little Fraud," Salon.com, December 20, 2001.

Bledsoe, Bob. "Book reviews," *Tulsa World*, December 5, 1990.

Browder, Laura. *Slippery Characters: Ethnic Impersonators and American Identities*. The University of North Carolina Press, Chapel Hill, 2000.

———. Telephone interview with author, December 15, 2008.

Carter, Dan T. *The Politics of Rage: George Wallace, the Origins of the New Conservatism, and the Transformation of American Politics*. Simon & Schuster, New York, 1995.

———. "Southern History, American Fiction: The Secret Life of Southwestern Novelist Forrest Carter," *Rewriting the South: History and Fiction*. Francke, Tübingen, Germany, 1993.

———. "The Transformation of a Klansman," *The New York Times*, October 4, 1991.

Carter, Forrest. *The Education of Little Tree*. University of New Mexico Press, Albuquerque, 2004.

———. *Gone to Texas*. Delacorte Press, New York, 1975.

Davis, Dick. "The Little Tree in Forrest," *Writer's Digest*, May 1977.

Donahue, Deirdre. "'Little Tree' grows into a best seller," *USA Today*, October 1, 1991.

Gates, Henry Louis Jr. "'Authenticity,' or the Lesson of Little Tree," *The New York Times*, November 24, 1991.

Gluck, Robert L. "Little House in the Mountains," *The Washington Post*, August 5, 1990.

Gone to Texas: The Lives of Forrest Carter. Written by Laura Browder.

Directed by Douglas Newman and Marco Ricci. ITVS, 2010. Incomplete edit on DVD.

"Is Forrest Carter Really Asa Carter? Only Josey Wales May Know for Sure," *The New York Times*, August 26, 1976.

Lee, Felicia R. "Best Seller Is a Fake, Professor Asserts," *The New York Times*, October 4, 1991.

McDowell, Edwin. "Book Notes," *The New York Times*, February 27, 1991.

———. "Book Notes," *The New York Times*, April 24, 1991.

Menninger, Karl. "Reading notes," *Bulletin of the Menninger Clinic*, Fall 1990.

Moynihan, Mary M. Book review of *The Education of Little Tree*, *Teaching Sociology*, January 1991.

Reid, Calvin. "Widow of 'Little Tree' Author Admits He Changed Identity," *Publishers Weekly*, October 25, 1991.

Roche, Jeff. "Asa/Forrest Carter and Regional/Political Identity," *The Southern Albatross: Race and Ethnicity in the American South*. Mercer University Press, Macon, Georgia, 1999.

Rubin, Dana. "The Real Education of Little Tree," *Texas Monthly*, February 1992.

St. John, Bob. "Little Tree's spirit lives on in best seller," *The Dallas Morning News*, September 17, 1991.

Stansberry, Rhonda. "Good Books Impact Young Imaginations," *The Omaha World-Herald*, June 18, 1991.

PRINCESS CARABOO

Borsay, Peter. *The Image of Georgian Bath, 1700–2000: Towns, Heritage, and History*. Oxford University Press, Oxford, England, 2000.

Gutch, John Matthew. *Caraboo: A Narrative of a Singular Imposition, Practised Upon the Benevolence of a Lady Residing in the Vicinity of the City of Bristol, by a Young Woman of the Name of Mary Willcocks, alias Baker, alias Bakerstendht, alias Caraboo, Princess of Javasu*. Baldwin, Cradock and Joy, London, 1817.

"The Princess Caraboo," *Trewman's Exeter Flying-Post*, January 25, 1865.

Spaughton, Bernard. Correspondence with author, August 2, 2008.

———. "Princess Caraboo," accessed at http://www.btinternet .com/~b.spaughton/caraboo.html on November 19, 2009.

Wells, John. *Princess Caraboo: Her True Story.* Pan Books, London, 1994.

Wilkinson, C. H. "The Unknown Foreigner," *Trewman's Exeter Flying-Post*, June 12, 1817.

ELLEN CRAFT

Blackett, R. J. M. *Beating Against the Barriers: Biographical Essays in Nineteenth-Century Afro-American History.* Louisiana State University Press, Baton Rouge, 1986.

Craft, William and Ellen Craft. *Running a Thousand Miles for Freedom.* University of Georgia Press, Athens, 1999.

Dilts, James. *The Great Road: The Building of the Baltimore & Ohio, the Nation's First Railroad, 1828–1853,* Stanford, California: Stanford University Press, 1993

Fradin, Judith Bloom and Dennis Brindell Fradin. *5,000 Miles to Freedom: Ellen and William Craft's Flight from Slavery.* National Geographic Society, Washington, D.C., 2006.

Harwood, Herbert H. Jr. *Impossible Challenge II: Baltimore to Washington and Harpers Ferry from 1828 to 1994.* Barnard, Roberts and Co., Baltimore, 1994.

Hendrick, George and Willene Hendrick, editors. *Fleeing for Freedom: Stories of the Underground Railroad As Told by Levi Coffin and William Still,* Chicago: Ivan R. Dee, 2004.

McCaskill, Barbara. "'Trust No Man!' But What about a Woman? Ellen Craft and a Genealogical Model for Teaching Douglass's *Narrative*," *Approaches to Teaching* Narrative of the Life of Frederick Douglass, James C. Hall, editor. The Modern Language Association of America, New York, 1999.

———. "'Yours Very Truly': Ellen Craft—The Fugitive as Text and Artifact," *African American Review*, Volume 28, Number 4, 1994.

McInnis, Maurie D. *The Politics of Taste in Antebellum Charleston.* The University of North Carolina Press, Chapel Hill, 2005.

Mencken, August. *The Railroad Passenger Car: An Illustrated History of the First Hundred Years with Accounts by Contemporary Passengers.* The Johns Hopkins Press, Baltimore, 1957.

Ripley, C. Peter, editor. *The Black Abolitionist Papers, Volume 1: The British Isles, 1830–1865*. The University of North Carolina Press, Chapel Hill, 1985.

Stover, John F. *History of the Baltimore and Ohio Railroad*. Purdue University Press, West Lafayette, Indiana, 1987.

Way, William. *The Old Exchange and Custom House*. Rebecca Motte Chapter, South Carolina Daughters of the American Revolution, Charleston, South Carolina, 1942.

White, John H. Jr. *The American Railroad Passenger Car*. The Johns Hopkins University Press, Baltimore, 1979.

JOHN HOWARD GRIFFIN

Baker, James T. "John Howard Griffin: Christian in Grease Paint," *The Christian Century*, December 22–29, 1982.

Bonazzi, Robert. Correspondence with author, October 16–20, 2008.

―――. *Man in the Mirror: John Howard Griffin and the Story of Black Like Me*. Orbis Books, Maryknoll, New York, 1997.

Cargas, Harry James. "A Christian Hero," *The Christian Century*, November 19, 1980.

Cook, Joan. "John H. Griffin Dead; White Novelist Wrote Book Black Like Me," *The New York Times*, September 10, 1980.

Griffin, John Howard. *Black Like Me: The Definitive Griffin Estate Edition*. Wings Press, San Antonio, 2006.

―――. *Scattered Shadows: A Memoir of Blindness and Vision*. Orbis Books, Maryknoll, New York, 2004.

Lott, Eric. "White Like Me: Racial Cross-Dressing and the Construction of American Whiteness," from *Cultures of United States Imperialism*, Amy Kaplan and Donald E. Pease, editors. Duke University Press, Durham, North Carolina, 1993.

Sharpe, Ernest Jr. "The Man Who Changed His Skin," *American Heritage Magazine*, February 1989.

RILEY WESTON

Adler, Jerry and Corie Brown with Esther Pan. "Teen Envy in Hollywood," *Newsweek*, October 26, 1998.

Axelman, Arthur. "She Fooled Us, but Don't Discount Her Writing," *Los Angeles Times*, November 2, 1998.

Chetwynd, Josh. "A success story too good to be true? Well, yes," *USA Today*, October 19, 1998.

Collins, Scott. "The 'kid' wants back in the picture; Riley Weston, who fell from sight after posing as a teen writer-actor, seeks a comeback," *Los Angeles Times*, December 20, 2004.

de Moraes, Lisa. "'Teen' Writer Sensation Has One Big Wrinkle," *The Washington Post*, October 16, 1998.

"Drawing the Line, Part 2." *Felicity: Freshman Year Collection (The Complete First Season)*. Writ. J. J. Abrams and Riley Weston. Dir. Joan Tewkesbury. Buena Vista Home Entertainment, 2002. DVD.

Epstein, Alex. *Crafty TV Writing: Thinking Inside the Box*. Henry Holt and Company, New York, 2006.

"Felicity Flap," *All Things Considered*, National Public Radio, October 16, 1998, transcript.

Flint, Joe. "The Life Of Riley; 32-year-old writer pretended to be 19 and wowed the cast and crew of 'Felicity' with her talent," *Entertainment Weekly*, October 30, 1998.

Ford, Luke. Interview with Riley Weston, October 16, 2007. Accessed at http://www.lukeford.net/profiles/profiles/rileyweston.htm on November 19, 2009.

Hontz, Jenny. "Old enough to know better; Writer created new teen ID for herself," *Variety*, October 15, 1998.

———. "Older, chastened Weston speaks out; Writer: 'age problem' contributed to ruse," *Variety*, October 16, 1998.

———. Telephone interview with author, January 4, 2010.

Lowry, Brian. "32-Year-Old Actress-Writer Admits Lying About Being 19," *Los Angeles Times*, October 16, 1998.

Pope, Kyle. "Hollywood Falls for 'Teen' Scribe's Tall Story," *The Wall Street Journal*, October 16, 1998.

"Riley Weston," The Internet Movie Database (http://www.imdb.com/name/nm0923005/), accessed November 19, 2009.

"Riley Weston: The Life of Riley," *Entertainment Weekly*, June 19, 1998.

Weinraub, Bernard. "The Girl Who Faked Out Hollywood and Then Got Caught," *Cosmopolitan*, January 1999.

"The Young and the Restless," *60 Minutes*, CBS, February 21, 1999. Television.

Zeman, Ned. "Youth or consequences," *Vanity Fair*, January 1999.

FRANK W. ABAGNALE JR.

20/20, ABC, November 22, 2002. Television.

Abagnale, Frank W. Address, National Automobile Dealers Association Convention, February 12, 2006. Accessed at http://www.americanrhetoric.com/speeches/frankabagnalenada2006.htm on November 19, 2009.

———. Correspondence with author, October 23, 2009.

———. Telephone interview with author, July 30, 2008.

——— with Stan Redding. *Catch Me If You Can*. Broadway Books, New York, 2002.

Baker, Bob. "Keeping it real; A con man's story leads our hero to new heights of second-guessing," Bob Baker's NewsThinking. Accessed at http://www.newsthinking.com/post-rehab-ii-keeping-it-real/ on November 19, 2009.

Rehm, Diane. Interview with Frank Abagnale, *The Diane Rehm Show*, WAMU 88.5 FM, Washington, DC, May 21, 2007.

Swan, Norman. "Frank Abagnale—New Life," *Life Matters*, Australian Broadcasting Corporation Radio National, March 17, 2000.

Tennant, Don. "Q&A: Former fraudster Frank Abagnale offers IT security advice; Nobody cares about ethics, says the Catch Me If You Can man," *Computerworld*, October 18, 2007.